LEITH'S COOKING FOR ONE OR TWO

LEITH'S COOKING FOR ONE OR TWO

POLLY TYRER

FOREWORD BY
CAROLINE
WALDEGRAVE

PHOTOGRAPHS BY GRAHAM KIRK

BLOOMSBURY

First published in Great Britain in 1996
Bloomsbury Publishing Plc, 2 Soho Square, London W1V 6HB

Copyright © 1996 Leith's School of Food and Wine

The moral right of the author has been asserted

A CIP catalogue record for this book is available from the British Library

ISBN 0 7475 2724 5

10 9 8 7 6 5 4 3 2 1

Typeset by Hewer Text Composition Services, Edinburgh
Printed by The Bath Press, Bath

Photographer: Graham Kirk
Stylist: Helen Payne

CONTENTS

ACKNOWLEDGEMENTS

I am particularly grateful to Debbie Major for her advice and guidance throughout the writing of this book. Most of the egg and soup sections were developed by Debbie.

I would like to thank Leith's School of Food and Wine for their support, especially that of Caroline Waldegrave. Thanks also to Jenny Kieldsen for advice and assistance with recipe testing; W & G Software for printing my manuscript; Richard Harvey for his recommendations on keeping wine; and the many friends who patiently consumed my trials and errors, among them Jackie, Gerry, Karen, Chris and Tony.

Finally, special thanks to my husband, children and mother for putting up with me over the last six months.

FOREWORD

Most cookery books assume that there are always going to be four people at every meal. Here, at last, is one that takes cooking for one, or possibly two, seriously. The recipes are naturally fairly simple, as few people are likely to spend hours over a hot stove cooking just for themselves. Some of the ideas, however, are very sophisticated, such as duck with honey and orange salsa, quails braised with cabbage and plums, grilled lamb with minted aubergines, and chocolate truffle pots. There are also some deliciously indulgent recipes for those days when comfort feels just right.

Polly has also included much useful, practical advice on shopping, getting organized, unusual ingredients and kitchen equipment. Last, but far from least, the wine section offers suggestions on what to drink with different types of food, and explains how to use a wine saver.

I do hope that you enjoy cooking from this book.

CAROLINE WALDEGRAVE

INTRODUCTION

INTRODUCTION

There is a widely held view that cooking for one or two is the exception rather than the general rule. Yet, if you look at everyday habits, we spend most of our lives providing for no more than two – first on leaving home, inexperienced and usually surviving on a shoe-string, and later when out to work and setting up a first home. The early years of parenthood are spent providing for small children and adults separately, and growing children have such full after-school diaries that the need to provide meals in shifts continues even then. There may be a brief period before the children become teenagers when we dine *en famille*, but then we are back to cooking for one or two. In fact, traditional family cooking never impinges on some people: one-parent families and those living alone form a growing percentage of our population.

This book is for people who enjoy cooking and are sensitive to the pleasures of delicious, healthy eating and the feeling of well-being that this promotes. Even hard-core convenience food consumers may be inspired by many of the recipes in this book as they can be prepared in the same amount of time as it takes to reheat a chilled meal.

Leith's Cooking for One or Two is about everyday eating. What most of us want is to prepare fresh, healthy food with the minimum of fuss and bother. Consequently, the recipes are simple and selected to cover eating on a budget, traditional dishes, modern grilled meats, salads, snacks, puddings and a few luxury items for treats – a collection of old favourites and new ideas. Some thought has been given to ingredients so that shopping can be kept to a minimum, and also to washing up. There is nothing more dampening to the spirits than a sinkful of dirty dishes to tackle alone, or, worse still, after a romantic supper for two. Many of the recipes produce a complete meal from a single pot.

There is practical information too: tips on cooking in bulk and freezing, how to shop in small doses and suggestions for practical kitchen equipment. There is also a section on how to keep wine once opened – after all, eating solo does not require temperance, whatever may be said about drinking alone.

Here is an opportunity to experiment and enjoy the art of cooking without the chore of preparing great quantities.

ORGANIZATION

ORGANIZATION

Being organized sounds rather a chore. However, there is no doubt that a little energy invested in thoughtful shopping is rewarded later on.

Good-quality, fresh ingredients are the basis of good cooking. When catering for one or two, buy fresh ingredients in small quantities; keep a well-stocked store cupboard so that there is always a meal to be put together if all else fails; use specialist shops for unusual ingredients. Mail-order shopping is very useful for people who live in areas bereft of specialist suppliers.

It is possible to shop once a week at the supermarket topped up with an occasional visit to the greengrocer, fishmonger or butcher. Nowadays, supermarkets can meet almost every need, offering an outstanding choice of foods from all over the world. The trick is to use supermarkets for what they are best at and to supplement their supplies from elsewhere. Use delicatessens or the deli counters of supermarkets for buying cold meats, cheese and olives in small quantities.

Pay some respect to seasons. Even though much produce is now available all year round, this does not mean that it is at its best. Check produce, especially exotic fruit, for ripeness. A hard mango, for example, can take up to a week to ripen. Local greengrocers may stock locally grown fruit and vegetables, and they usually have considerably riper and better-tasting tomatoes than supermarkets.

Be organized about freezing: keeping a sensibly stocked freezer can be a great time-saver and avoid multiple shopping trips. Such things as interesting bread, peas, spinach, fresh-filled pasta, chicken thighs, turkey breast or ice-cream all freeze well and are good standbys.

Recipes suitable for freezing are indicated throughout. Prepare them in bulk and freeze in individual portions. Food to be frozen should be cooled as quickly as possible and frozen immediately. Defrost thoroughly before reheating and heat until piping hot all the way through.

Make casseroles the day before needed then cool, cover and chill overnight. This gives the flavours time to mingle. Many recipes in this book make use of marinades, so do cast a thought the day before as to what tomorrow's supper might be. Marinating dishes overnight greatly improves the flavour and, in some cases, helps to tenderize meat. This routine makes for a quick meal the next day when all that needs to be done is to fry or grill the marinated food.

FOOD SAFETY

FOOD SAFETY

These are the most important factors to take into account
for food safety.

1. Bugs like warmth, moisture and to be left undisturbed, so try not to give them these ideal conditions.

2. Keep cooking utensils and hands clean. Change J-cloths, tea towels and washing-up brushes regularly.

3. Store raw meat at the bottom of the refrigerator so that any meat juices cannot drip on to cooked food.

4. Wrap food up loosely, let it breathe.

5. Don't put hot food into the refrigerator – it will raise the temperature. Refrigerators should be kept at 5°C.

6. Get food to cool down as quickly as possible.

7. Never cover cooling hot food.

8. Avoid cross-contamination of germs – store raw and cooked foods separately as far as possible. If you mix raw and cooked foods, they should both be cold and then reheated thoroughly.

Avoid keeping food warm for any length of time: it should be either hot or cold.

9. Never cook large items (e.g. whole chickens) from frozen.

10. Salmonella in eggs: consumption of raw eggs or uncooked dishes made from them, such as home-made mayonnaise, mousse and ice-cream, carries the risk of food poisoning. If you do use raw eggs, make sure that you use only the freshest (pasteurized eggs are available), that the dishes are eaten as soon as possible after making and that they are never left for more than 1 hour at room temperature.

Vulnerable people such as the elderly, the sick, babies, toddlers and pregnant women should only eat eggs that have been thoroughly cooked until both white and yolk are solid.

INGREDIENTS

INGREDIENTS

Balsamic vinegar is made from grape juice which has undergone a lengthy fermentation and ageing process. It has a rich, sweet flavour and is well worth the investment. Choose a mid-priced vinegar from a delicatessen as cheaper balsamic vinegars are harsh. Add to sauces and dressings.

Chillies seem to be almost addictive. Once in the habit of using them, it is difficult to stop! The chillies referred to in this book are fresh and are the milder variety mostly found in supermarkets. As a general rule, the smaller the chilli the hotter it is. Red chillies are riper and sweeter than green. Don't be afraid to experiment; chillies are not always as fiery as their reputation and provide a distinct flavour as well as heat. The seeds can be cooked but are seriously hot. Take care when preparing chillies that you do not touch your face or eyes after handling them.

Creamed coconut This is bought in a hard block and needs to be chopped or dissolved in boiling water before use. It is a very useful thickening agent if added to sauces at the end of cooking. Look out for the packets containing two 55g/2oz sachets which are perfect for cooking in small quantities.

Crème fraîche is a cultured cream and thus has a faintly sour flavour. It has a minimum fat content of 35 per cent, which makes it ideal for adding to sauces without fear of curdling. It is also excellent to serve with desserts and has a longer shelf life than double or single cream. All in all, it is a very useful ingredient for lone cooks.

Curry leaves These look like small bay leaves and have a mild, curry-like scent. They are available fresh from Indian shops or can be found dried, whole or powdered in supermarkets.

Feta is a white Greek cheese ripened in brine, so it has a sharp, salty taste.

Fish sauce may be also labelled by its Thai name 'Nam pla'. This is a dark, salty sauce, rather like soy, but with a distinct fishy kick. It is used as a seasoning throughout Southeast Asia and can be found nearer home in specialist shops or major supermarkets.

Fresh herbs It is wonderful to have enough fresh herbs to use in generous quantities. Grow your own, if possible, or buy small pots of them from a supermarket. These are especially useful for cooking in small quantities and will keep growing for some time if carefully looked after. Small cartons of frozen, chopped fresh herbs can also be bought and are very convenient for scattering in hot dishes.

Greek yoghurt is a thick, full-fat yoghurt. Always buy the sort that is strained. This yoghurt is delicious enough to serve alone as a dessert, but may also be topped with honey or added to soups and sauces.

Lemon grass is the essence of Southeast Asian cooking. It is sold in stalks and can be bought from Oriental food shops or major supermarkets. To prepare: remove the outer layer and crush the stem with the flat side of a knife. Chop the lower part but use the tougher top half whole, for flavouring soups, stocks or rice. Remove at the end of cooking.

Mustard Keep two sorts in store: English, either as powder or paste, and a milder mustard such as Dijon or wholegrain.

Oils Keep a bottle of sunflower oil and a bottle of good-quality olive oil in your store cupboard. As an indulgence, a bottle of walnut or hazelnut oil is worth having for salad dressings and warm salads, as is sesame oil for making stir-fries. Store away from direct light.

Pancetta is Italian streaky bacon. It has a particularly pungent flavour. Be sure to buy it in a lump (rather than thinly sliced) for dicing. Available diced in two 65g sealed portions which keep for up to 6 weeks.

Parmesan cheese, or more correctly Parmigiano Reggiano, is a hard Italian cheese. The sort bought ready-grated in small drums tastes of very little, so buy the cheese in a block: grate half and keep refrigerated in a jar. Save the rest for 'shavings'.

Part-baked bread can be stored in the freezer and cooked from frozen. This is almost as good as fresh bread and makes the perfect accompaniment to a rustic supper.

Passata is simply puréed and sieved tomatoes. This is a very useful base for casseroles, sauces and soups, and can also be used as a quick pizza sauce. It is available only in large bottles, so freeze any unused passata in small quantities for future use.

Pesto Green pesto is a thick paste of basil leaves, pine kernels, Parmesan, garlic and oil. Red pesto is a similar mixture, but contains sun-dried tomatoes rather than basil. Pesto is traditionally served with pasta but is also a useful condiment. Store it in airtight jars, scraping any excess from the sides and floating a little olive oil on top.

Pinenuts are also known as pine kernels. They have a rich, creamy flavour which is enhanced by toasting or frying, but they burn very quickly, so beware. Buy them in small quantities as the high oil content soon turns rancid and ruins the flavour.

Soy sauce There are two main varieties: light soy sauce is pale in colour, thin and very salty; dark soy sauce is heavier, sweeter and can be used as a dipping sauce. Japanese shoyu is light and generally sweeter and less salty than light soy sauce.

Stock Use home-made stock whenever possible (see pages 162–163). The next best thing is chilled stock available from supermarkets. This can be stored in the freezer.

Sun-dried tomatoes are halved tomatoes left to dry in the sun until shrivelled and deeply concentrated in flavour. They have been the fashionable ingredient of the 1990s, so they are now easily available. Buy them dried, stored in oil or as a paste. If using the dried variety, reconstitute them by soaking in boiling water for 2 hours before using. Use in sandwiches and salads, or chop them and add to sauces, casseroles and pasta dishes.

Sweet potatoes have white or orange flesh with a sweet, nutty flavour. Like ordinary potatoes, they can be baked in their skins and served with butter. Alternatively, they make good 'oven chips' if sliced, tossed in oil and baked in a hot oven until charred on the outside.

TECHNIQUES

TECHNIQUES

Peeling tomatoes Douse in boiling water for 10 seconds. Carefully split the skin with a sharp knife. It will now peel away easily.

Deglazing Using stock or water to loosen the sticky juices left at the bottom of a pan after frying meat or fish.

Reducing Rapidly boiling liquid to reduce the quantity and increase the flavour. This is a useful technique for thickening sauces.

Marinating Soaking meat, fish or vegetables in an acidulated liquid containing flavourings and herbs. This adds flavour and tenderizes.

Cleaning squid Pull the head and tentacles from the body. Cut off the tentacles and discard the head and entrails. Wash the body, scraping off the skin with a sharp knife. Remove the 'pen' (clear cartilage) from the bag.

Filleting mackerel Remove the head. Slit open the belly and rinse out, removing any entrails. Lay the fish cut side down and press firmly down the length of the backbone with a thumb. Turn the fish over. The backbone should now lift easily from the flesh. Cook the fish whole or cut into two fillets.

Deveining prawns Check the prawns for a black vein running down the back and remove it with a sharp knife. This is usually necessary for large and uncooked prawns.

Pin boning This should be done with all cuts of fish before cooking to remove the small, irritating bones that run along the flanks of fish. Run the fingertips of one hand over the surface of the flesh to locate the ends of the small bones, then pull them out with tweezers or pliers. The fish is now ready for cooking.

EQUIPMENT

EQUIPMENT

The best kitchen equipment is simple and sturdy. The cooking techniques in this book do not require anything fancy. However, there is no doubt that a pie looks more appetizing if cooked in the right sized pie dish and that a stew simmers to succulent perfection in the right sized saucepan. There are a few items of equipment that will help to achieve the best results quickly.

Knives Good sharp knives are a must. We suggest an 18cm/7 inch carbon steel chopping knife, a 7.5cm/3 inch stainless steel fruit/vegetable knife, a palette knife and a serrated bread knife (cutting bread with a kitchen knife will dull the blade).

Saucepans A 1.4 litre/2½ pint pan and two 860ml/1½ pint pans should cover most needs.

Ovenproof dishes A 290ml/½ pint dish is ideal for one serving, and a 570ml/1 pint dish holds enough for two.

Omelette pans Have a 15cm/6 inch cast-iron or non-stick pan.

Sauté pan or wok This is essential for stir-frying.

Very heavy-based frying pan This is needed for browning and pan-frying meat. Choose one about 20cm/8 inches in diameter. Cast-iron griddles, either plain or with a ridged base, produce a reasonably authentic char-grilled flavour. If grilled meats, fish, vegetables or breads feature prominently in your cooking, a griddle might be a luxury

worth considering. Remember, though, that pan sauces cannot be made on a griddle.

Electric mixer These can be mounted on a stand or hand-held. Use with only one beater when mixing small quantities.

Food processor This is essential for speeding up laborious chores such as making soups, breadcrumbs and mayonnaise. Choose a small machine as large ones do not function properly when processing small amounts.

Coffee grinder While this is necessary for producing freshly ground coffee, it is also essential for making ground spice mixes. Note, however, that it is not a good idea to use one machine for both purposes as cleaning is difficult and the flavour of one ingredient will taint the other.

Combination microwave/convector oven In recent years the quality of these ovens has improved tremendously and they are now extremely sophisticated pieces of kitchen equipment. The oven, which is the size of a large microwave, will microwave only, convect only, or do both at the same time. The advantage of this is that microwaved food can be cooked quickly *and* have a crisp brown exterior. The convection function is even and efficient and most ovens are equipped with grills. While combination ovens are not big enough to cope with cooking Christmas lunch or to deal with large quantities of baking, they are the ideal choice for people cooking for small numbers.

Microwave ovens These are good for cooking certain foods and are generally a useful cooking accessory. As the microwaves work on the liquid content of food, cooking continues after microwaving stops, so standing time is often necessary. Microwaves are particularly good for cooking vegetables, especially sweetcorn, carrots, courgettes, baked potatoes and mangetout, soups and fish, melting butter and browning onions. Use for defrosting only in an emergency as the food will lose a lot of moisture during the process.

STORING WINE

STORING WINE

There are not too many options when buying wine in small quantities. Wines offered in cans or tetra paks tend to be inferior to those in bottles.

If drinking quality wine is the aim, half bottles are a good choice and just about the right quantity to accompany a meal. This, however, is an expensive option as half bottles cost more than half the price of a full bottle.

The problems associated with opening full bottles of wine and keeping them once opened depend on how much is drunk in one sitting. Assuming most of us drink moderately, catering for one or two will sometimes mean that there is a little leftover wine to be stored.

Wine will keep happily overnight if it is simply corked – white, stored in the refrigerator, and red, in a cool place.

If wine is to be kept for longer, there are certain gadgets that will help preserve it. A 'Wine Saver', for example, sprays an inert gas into the bottle. This forms a blanket over the wine and prevents it oxidizing, which spoils the flavour. A 'Vacu Vin' is a little pump, which removes air from the bottle, creating a vacuum and thus also preventing oxidization.

Red wine tends to keep better than white, but it's best not to keep any opened wine longer than 3–4 days.

With luck, we may soon see the 50cl bottles of wine that have become so popular in France. These provide two-thirds of the quantity found in a full bottle and are fitted with a screw top. Don't let the screw top put you off – it provides a good seal and is no longer an indication of inferior-quality wine.

Do remember that small amounts of leftover wine can be frozen in cubes and used in soups and stews.

SOUPS

SOUPS

Soup makes a very good snack, lunch or even a main course if served with a side dish. Most vegetables can be made into soup by cooking them in stock with onion for flavour and potato for thickening. In fact, soups are a great way of using up any leftover vegetables.

Accompaniments: grissini sticks, crusty bread or crackers
Toppings: Greek yoghurt, cream, grated cheese, croûtons, fresh herbs
To serve as a main meal: add dumplings (see page 169), bruschetta (see page 168), a baked potato (see page 148), a toasted filled baguette or doorstep sandwich.

The quantities given in the basic recipe below are only a rough guide. Don't worry too much if you have a little more or less of anything. Any vegetable or combination of vegetables can be used. If you intend to freeze the soup, do so at the end of step 1 and add the milk while reheating.

All recipes serve 1 unless stated otherwise.

BASIC SOUP RECIPE

SERVES 2
½ medium onion, sliced
1 medium potato, peeled and diced
prepared vegetables, such as 1 leek; 2 carrots; 1 bunch watercress, stalks removed; huge handful of lettuce; 1 parsnip; 6 celery stalks; cauliflower or broccoli florets
290ml/½ pint chicken or vegetable stock (see page 162–163)
salt and freshly ground black pepper
about 150ml/¼ pint creamy milk, or cream

1. Put the onion, potato and vegetables into a large saucepan. Pour in the stock and season with salt and pepper. Simmer for 30–40 minutes until all the vegetables are very tender. Alternatively, put the mixture into a covered microwave container and microwave on high for 20 minutes.
2. Liquidize or process the mixture until very smooth. Reheat, adding milk to thin the soup to the desired consistency.

MINESTRONE WITH PARMESAN DUMPLINGS

This soup is more of a meal than a soup!

SERVES 2
1 tablespoon olive oil
½ medium-sized onion, peeled and sliced
1 garlic clove, crushed
1 carrot, peeled
1 celery stick
1 courgette
350ml/12 fl oz chicken or vegetable stock (see page 162–163)
30g/1oz dried green flageolet beans, soaked overnight
1 × 225g/8oz tin tomatoes
1 teaspoon dried basil
dash tomato purée
salt and freshly ground black pepper
1 tablespoon frozen leaf spinach
15g/½oz broken spaghetti or about 8 chilled cappeletti, tortelloni or ravioli
2 quantities dumplings (see page 169)

To serve:
Parmesan cheese

1. Heat the oil in a heavy-based saucepan. Add the onion and fry gently until soft and transparent. Add the garlic and fry for a further minute.
2. Meanwhile, chop the carrot, celery and courgette into 1cm/½ inch chunks. Add to the pan, then cover and cook gently for 5 minutes until the vegetables are soft.
3. Pour in the stock and add the flageolets, tomatoes, basil and tomato purée. Season with salt and ground black pepper. Simmer for 45 minutes until the beans are tender.
4. Add the spinach and pasta to the mixture and bring back to the boil.
5. Drop the dumpling mixture in two spoonfuls into the simmering soup. Cover and cook for 10 minutes, then uncover and cook for a further 10 minutes. Serve with a sprinkling of Parmesan cheese.

TIP: Make double the quantity of this soup and freeze half at the end of step 3. To use, defrost, bring up to boiling point and continue as described in steps 4 and 5.

CHUNKY BEETROOT AND CUMIN SOUP

225g/8oz small uncooked beetroot
15g/½oz butter
½ small onion, finely chopped
½ teaspoon ground cumin
¾ pint vegetable stock (see page 163)
2 teaspoons freshly squeezed lemon juice
1 tablespoon medium dry sherry
salt and freshly ground black pepper

For the garnish:
1 tablespoon soured cream
1 teaspoon chopped fresh chives

1. Peel the beetroot and cut into 1cm/½ inch dice.
2. Melt the butter in a pan. Add the onion and cook over medium heat for 5 minutes until soft but not browned.
3. Add the cumin and cook for 30 seconds. Add the beetroot and stock, then cover and simmer for 25 minutes.
4. Stir the lemon juice and sherry into the soup and season to taste. Simmer for 5 minutes. Decorate with the soured cream and chopped chives.

❋ Suitable for freezing at the end of stage 3.

SUMMER GARDEN SOUP

3 spring onions, trimmed
110g/4oz small courgettes
2 plum tomatoes, peeled
½ tablespoon olive oil
425ml/¾ pint vegetable stock (see page 163)
½ teaspoon sun-dried or ordinary tomato purée
15g/½oz watercress leaves, washed
1 teaspoon chopped tarragon
salt and freshly ground black pepper

To serve:
green pesto
foccacia bread

1. Thinly slice the spring onions. Trim the courgettes and slice. Finely chop the tomatoes.
2. Heat the oil in a pan. Add the spring onions and cook for 1 minute. Add the courgettes and cook for 1 minute.
3. Add the tomatoes, stock and tomato purée to the pan. Cover and simmer for 10 minutes.
4. Meanwhile, finely chop the watercress. Add to the soup with the tarragon and season to taste. Simmer for 2 minutes. Serve with a swirl of pesto and warm foccacia bread.

LENTIL AND PARMA HAM SOUP

This soup is very good served with tomato and basil bruschetta (see page 168) or hot grilled sausages sandwiched in a chunk of French bread.

½ small onion
1 small carrot, peeled
1 celery stick
½ tablespoon olive oil
1 small garlic clove, crushed
45g/1½oz dried green or brown lentils
570ml/1 pint vegetable stock (see page 163)
30g/1oz Parma ham, chopped
1 teaspoon chopped parsley
salt and freshly ground black pepper

1. Finely chop the onion, carrot and celery. Heat the oil in a pan, add the vegetables, cover and cook over a medium heat for 5 minutes.
2. Add the garlic and cook for 1 minute. Add the lentils and stock, bring to the boil and simmer for 20–25 minutes.
3. Add the Parma ham, parsley and seasoning to taste. Cover and simmer for 1 minute.

❋ Suitable for freezing.

CREAMY 'FISH PIE' SOUP

170g/6oz smoked haddock fillet, skinned
290ml/½ pint milk
½ bay leaf
15g/½oz butter
1 small leek, thinly sliced
15g/½oz plain flour
150ml/¼ pint vegetable stock (see page 163)
55g/2oz cooked peeled prawns
1 teaspoon freshly squeezed lemon juice
1 teaspoon chopped dill
1 teaspoon chopped parsley
2 tablespoons single cream
salt and freshly ground black pepper

For the garnish:
chopped parsley

1. Put the haddock, milk and bay leaf into a pan and slowly bring to the boil. Cover and simmer for 5 minutes.
2. Lift the fish out of the milk on to a plate and leave to cool slightly. Flake the fish, discarding the skin and bones. Set aside.
3. Strain the milk through a fine sieve into a jug. Melt half the butter in a clean pan, add the leek and cook for 2–3 minutes until soft but not browned. Lift out and set aside with the haddock.
4. Melt the remaining butter in the pan, stir in the flour and cook for 1 minute. Gradually stir in the reserved milk and the stock and bring slowly to the boil, stirring all the time. Reduce the heat and leave to simmer for 2 minutes.
5. Stir the flaked fish, leek, prawns, lemon juice, dill, parsley and cream into the soup. Season to taste and simmer for 2 minutes. Sprinkle with the chopped parsley and serve.

ROASTED RED PEPPER AND TOMATO SOUP

1 small red pepper
1 small red onion
3 plum tomatoes
1 tablespoon olive oil
1 garlic clove, unpeeled
425ml/¾ pint vegetable stock (see page 163)
½ teaspoon sun-dried tomato paste or red pesto
leaves from 1 small sprig fresh oregano or a pinch of dried
pinch caster sugar
salt and freshly ground black pepper
1 tablespoon chopped fresh basil

For the garnish:
few whole basil leaves

1. Heat the oven to 220°C/425°F/gas mark 7. Cut the red pepper in half, discard the seeds and membranes from inside, then chop the flesh into small chunks. Peel and slice the onion and quarter the tomatoes. Mix together in a bowl with the olive oil and the unpeeled clove of garlic.

2. Spread the vegetables out on a small baking tray and roast in the oven for 20–25 minutes, turning over now and then, until slightly blackened around the edges.

3. Lift out the garlic clove and put the rest of the roasted vegetables into a pan. Split open the skin of the garlic and squeeze the soft pulp into the pan. Add the stock, tomato purée, oregano and

sugar. Season to taste, then cover and simmer for 15 minutes.

4. Pour the soup into a liquidizer or food processor and blend until smooth. Press through a sieve back into the rinsed-out pan, check the seasoning and, if serving hot, bring slowly back to the boil. Stir in the chopped basil and garnish with the basil leaves before serving.

NOTE: This soup is also wonderful served cold. Pour the liquidized mixture into a bowl, then cover and chill for at least 6 hours or overnight. Stir in the basil just before serving, garnished with a couple of ice cubes and the basil sprigs.

❄ *Suitable for freezing.*

CAULIFLOWER CHEESE AND MUSTARD SOUP

15g/½oz butter
½ small onion, finely chopped
2 teaspoons plain flour
290ml/½ pint vegetable stock (see page 163)
110g/4oz cauliflower
150ml/¼ pint milk
2 tablespoons single cream (optional)
1 teaspoon Dijon mustard
55g/2oz Cheddar cheese, grated
2 teaspoons chopped chives
salt and freshly ground black pepper

1. Melt the butter in a pan. Add the onion and cook for 5 minutes until soft but not browned.
2. Add the flour and cook for 1 minute, stirring. Gradually add the stock, return to the heat and bring back to the boil, stirring all the time. Cut the cauliflower into small florets, add to the pan, then cover and simmer gently for 15 minutes.
3. Lift out half of the cauliflower florets and set aside. Pour the rest of the soup into a liquidizer or food processor and blend until smooth.
4. Pour the soup back into the pan and add the milk, cream (if using), mustard, cheese, half the chopped chives and the reserved cauliflower. Heat gently for 5 minutes, stirring until the cheese has melted. (Don't allow the soup to boil or the cheese will go stringy.) Season and garnish with the remaining chives.

CARROT AND GINGER SOUP

1 teaspoon sunflower oil
15g/½oz butter
½ small onion, finely chopped
2.5cm/1 inch piece fresh root ginger, peeled and finely grated
1 small garlic clove, crushed
½ teaspoon demerara sugar
225g/8oz carrots, peeled and diced
425ml/¾ pint vegetable stock (see page 163)
salt and freshly ground black pepper
1 tablespoon chopped fresh coriander

To serve:
hot buttered naan bread

1. Heat the oil and butter in a pan. Add the onion, ginger and demerara sugar. Cook over a low heat for 10 minutes until browned and slightly caramelized. Add the garlic and cook for 1 minute.
2. Add the carrots and stock to the pan and season to taste. Bring to the boil, cover and simmer for another 25–30 minutes or until the carrots are very soft.
3. Pour the soup into a liquidizer or food processor, add the coriander and blend until smooth. Serve with the naan bread.

❄ *Suitable for freezing.*

NO-COOK AVOCADO SOUP

1 small, ripe avocado
30g/1oz Boursin or garlic and herb
cheese
2 teaspoons lemon juice
290ml/½ pint cold chicken stock (see
page 162)
1–2 tablespoons single cream
few drops Tabasco sauce
salt and freshly ground black pepper

To serve
tomato salsa (see page 161)

1. Halve the avocado and remove the stone. Remove and discard the peel and put the flesh into a liquidizer or food processor with the Boursin and lemon juice. Turn on the machine and gradually add the stock until the mixture is smooth.
2. Pour the mixture into a bowl and stir in the cream. Add a few drops of Tabasco and season to taste. Add a little more lemon juice if necessary. Cover and chill for 1–2 hours. Serve topped with a spoonful of tomato salsa.

CHILLED LIME AND WATERCRESS SOUP

15g/½oz butter
1 leek, white part only, thinly sliced
170g/6oz potato, peeled and diced
425ml/¾ pint chicken or vegetable stock
(see page 162–163)
salt and freshly ground black pepper
30g/1oz watercress, washed, large stalks
removed
2 teaspoons freshly squeezed lime juice
2 tablespoons single cream

For the garnish:
single cream
coarsely grated lime zest

1. Heat the butter in a small pan. Add the leek and potato, then cover and cook over a gentle heat for 5 minutes.
2. Add the stock and season to taste. Bring to the boil, cover and simmer for 15 minutes or until the potatoes are soft.
3. Add the watercress and simmer for 3 minutes. Pour the soup into a liquidizer or food processor and blend until smooth. Pour into a bowl and stir in the lime juice and cream. Check the seasoning, cover and chill for 3–4 hours. Serve garnished with the cream and lime zest.

NOTE: This soup can also be served hot. Reheat until almost boiling and serve with a whirl of cream topped with lime shreds.

GARLIC, NEW POTATO AND PEA SOUP

Lots of garlic it has, but over-garlicky it isn't because the flavour mellows with cooking

3 garlic cloves
225/8oz new potatoes
15g/½oz butter
425ml/¾ pint vegetable stock (see page 163)
2 teaspoons chopped parsley
1 teaspoon chopped dill
salt and freshly ground black pepper
110g/4oz peas, fresh if possible

For the garnish:
snipped dill leaves

To serve:
crusty bread

1. Peel the cloves of garlic and slice thinly. Wash the potatoes and cut into small chunks.
2. Melt the butter in a pan and add the garlic and potatoes. Cover and cook over a low heat for 10 minutes, shaking the pan every now and then to make sure nothing is sticking.
3. Add the stock and herbs and season to taste. Cover and simmer for 15 minutes.
4. Lift half the cooked potatoes out of the pan and set to one side. Pour the rest of the mixture into a liquidizer or food processor and blend until smooth.

5. Pour the blended soup back into the pan and add the cooked potatoes and peas. Cover and simmer for 5 minutes or until tender. Sprinkle with the dill leaves and serve with crusty bread.

MIDDLE EASTERN SPINACH AND LEMON SOUP

110g/4oz frozen leaf spinach, thawed
15g/½oz butter
1 small onion, finely chopped
1 teaspoon turmeric powder
1 strip lemon zest
1 tablespoon freshly squeezed lemon juice
425ml/¾ pint vegetable stock (see page 163)
salt and freshly ground black pepper

For the garnish:
1 tablespoon Greek yoghurt
lemon slice

1. Squeeze the excess water out of the spinach and roughly chop. Melt the butter in a pan, add the onion and cook gently for 5 minutes until soft.
2. Add the turmeric and cook, stirring, for 1 minute. Add the spinach, lemon zest, lemon juice, stock and seasoning. Bring to the boil, then cover and simmer for 20 minutes.
3. Remove the strip of zest from the soup, then pour the mixture into a liquidizer or food processor and blend until smooth. Return to the pan, bring back to the boil and serve decorated with the yoghurt and a slice of lemon.

HOT AND SOUR SOUP

85g/3oz raw, unpeeled prawns
425ml/¾ pint chicken stock (see page 162)
1 strip lime zest
2.5cm/1 inch piece lemon grass or 1 strip lemon zest
½ red chilli, seeded and thinly sliced (see page 15)
1 teaspoon light soy sauce
½ teaspoon finely chopped red chilli (see page 15)
pinch soft light brown sugar
1 teaspoon freshly squeezed lime or lemon juice
55g/2oz button mushrooms, very thinly sliced
1 spring onion, thinly sliced
1 teaspoon coarsely chopped coriander

To serve:
prawn crackers

1. Prepare the prawns (see page 21), reserving the shells. Put the shells into a pan with the stock, lime zest, lemon grass or lemon zest and sliced chilli. Bring to the boil, cover and simmer for 15 minutes.
2. Strain the stock into a clean pan. Add the soy sauce, chopped chilli, sugar and lime juice. Bring back to the boil, add the prawns, mushrooms and spring onion and simmer for 3 minutes. Stir in the coriander and hand the prawn crackers separately.

PEA AND LETTUCE SOUP

15g/½oz butter
½ small onion, finely chopped
225g/8oz petit pois or frozen peas
pinch caster sugar
salt and freshly ground black pepper
½ little gem lettuce, finely shredded
425ml/¾ pint chicken stock (see
page 162)
2–3 teaspoons chopped fresh chervil or
parsley
1–2 tablespoons double cream

1. Melt the butter in a pan. Add the onion and cook over a low heat for 5 minutes until soft but not browned.
2. Add the peas, sugar and season to taste. Cover and cook over a low heat for 5 minutes. Add the lettuce, then cover and cook for a further 5 minutes.
3. Add the stock, bring to the boil, then cover and simmer for 10 minutes. Pour into a liquidizer or food processor, add the chervil or parsley and blend until smooth. Pour the soup back into the rinsed-out pan, bring back to the boil and stir in the cream. Taste and season if necessary.

EGGS

EGGS

There is no nutritional difference between the many kinds of eggs now found on the supermarket shelf. 'Free range' indicates some quality of life for the hens and generally an improvement in flavour. Genuine farm eggs can sometimes be found in local greengrocers or butchers. Check carefully for sell-by dates and buy the freshest available: these will usually be found in shops that have a high turnover.
Eggs are best stored in a cool place or refrigerated, and kept in the box in which they have been bought.
All recipes serve 1 unless stated otherwise.

PIPERADE

This dish, from the Basque region in southwest France, is a cross between an omelette and scrambled eggs. It can be a vehicle for many fillings, such as peppers, bacon, ham, mushrooms, potatoes or prawns.

1 tablespoon olive oil
30g/1oz butter
1 small onion, thinly sliced
1 small red pepper, seeded and sliced
2 large eggs
salt and freshly ground black pepper
1 small garlic clove, crushed
1 fresh tomato, skinned, seeded and sliced
few fresh basil leaves

To serve:
olive oil bread (see page 168)

1. Heat the olive oil and half the butter in a non-stick saucepan. Add the onion and red pepper and cook over a medium-high heat for 5 minutes, stirring now and then, until lightly golden.
2. Meanwhile, break the eggs into a bowl, season to taste and lightly beat with a fork. Melt half the remaining butter in another pan. Add the eggs and cook over a medium heat, stirring all the time, until half set. Take off the heat, add the rest of the butter and continue stirring, returning to the heat briefly if necessary, until soft and creamy.
3. Add the garlic and tomato to the onion mixture and cook for 1 minute. Tear the basil leaves into small pieces. Stir the vegetables and basil into the scrambled eggs and serve with the olive oil bread.

SPINACH AND RAISIN EGGAH

This dish is from the Middle East and is more like a dish of vegetables set with egg than an egg omelette filled with a vegetable mixture. Leave to cool slightly before cutting into wedges and serving.

4 teaspoons olive oil
½ small onion, finely chopped
110g/4oz frozen leaf spinach, thawed
good pinch ground cumin
good pinch ground coriander
1 tablespoon raisins
30g/1oz Parmesan cheese, finely grated
2 large eggs, beaten
salt and freshly ground black pepper
1 tablespoon toasted pinenuts

1. Heat 2 teaspoons of the oil in a small, non-stick frying pan. Add the onion and cook for 5 minutes until soft and lightly golden.
2. Meanwhile, squeeze the excess water out of the spinach and coarsely chop. Add the cumin and coriander to the onion and cook for 1 minute. Add the spinach and cook for 1 minute.
3. Tip the onion and spinach mixture into a bowl and mix in the raisins, Parmesan cheese and eggs. Season to taste.
4. Wipe out the pan with absorbent paper. Add the remaining oil and when hot, pour in the eggah mixture. Sprinkle over the pinenuts and cook over medium heat for 8–10 minutes or until the base is golden brown and the eggah is set. Meanwhile, preheat the grill to high.
5. Slide the frying pan under the grill and cook the contents for 2 minutes until golden. Cool slightly, then cut into wedges to serve.

ROSTI EGGS

Rosti is a traditional Swiss potato cake. Cooked with eggs, it makes a substantial brunch, lunch or evening snack. Serve with fresh bread.

2 × 110g/4oz potatoes
salt and freshly ground black pepper
2 teaspoons olive oil
30g/1oz butter
2 large eggs

For the garnish:
chopped fresh parsley

1. Boil the potatoes in their skins for 10 minutes. Drain, cover with cold water and leave to go cold. (If the potatoes are left in the fridge overnight, all the better.)

2. Peel and coarsely grate the potatoes and season with a little salt and pepper. Heat half the oil and half the butter in a 17.5–20cm/7–8 inch frying pan. Add the potatoes and level the top with the back of a spoon. Fry over a gentle heat for 15 minutes or until golden. Don't cook over too high a heat or the bottom will brown before the potato on the inside has had a chance to cook.

3. Cover the pan with an inverted plate, hold the two together and turn over so that the rosti is now on the plate. Return the pan to the heat, add the rest of the oil and butter and, when hot, slide in the rosti. Break through the crust of the potatoes and pull back the mixture to make two 6cm/2½ inch holes. Break in the eggs and cook for another 15 minutes until the bottom of the rosti is golden and the eggs are set. Serve sprinkled with the chopped parsley.

FRIED EGGS

Heat 2 tablespoons of oil (sunflower, vegetable or olive) in a non-stick frying pan over a high heat. Break 2 eggs, one at a time, into a cup, then carefully slide into the hot fat. Reduce the heat slightly and fry, spooning some of the hot fat over the tops of the eggs, until the whites are set and the egg yolks are runny (or to your liking).

HUEVOS RANCHEROS

Literally 'ranch-style eggs', this Tex-Mex snack can be eaten at any time of day but is traditionally eaten at breakfast with refried beans. The tortillas used in this recipe are the thin Mexican variety, usually sold as 'flour tortillas' in most major supermarkets.

2 large eggs
1 flour tortilla
30g/1oz Cheddar cheese, grated
½ small avocado, sliced

For the tomato sauce:
4 teaspoons sunflower oil
½ small onion, finely chopped
½ green pepper, seeded and finely chopped
1 small garlic clove, crushed
½ teaspoon finely chopped red chilli (see page 15)

225g/8oz can chopped tomatoes
1 teaspoon chopped fresh oregano or ½ teaspoon dried oregano
salt and cayenne pepper

1. First make the tomato sauce: heat half the oil in a small pan. Add the onion and green pepper and cook for 5 minutes until soft. Add the garlic and chilli and fry for 2 minutes. Add the chopped tomatoes and oregano, season to taste and simmer for 10 minutes or until thickened. Keep hot over a low heat.
2. Add the remaining oil to the pan and heat. Break in the eggs and fry until just set. Meanwhile, heat a dry frying pan, add the tortilla and cook for 1 minute on each side until puffed up and lightly browned.
1. To serve, slide the tortilla on to a plate and spoon over the sauce. Top with the fried eggs and sprinkle with the grated cheese and avocado.

SOFTBOILED EGGS WITH ASPARAGUS TIPS

2 large eggs, at room temperature
6–8 asparagus tips
a little softened butter
salt and freshly ground black pepper

To serve:
wholemeal bread or toast

1. Pierce the blunt end of the eggs with a pin. Carefully lower them into a small pan of barely simmering water, cover and simmer for 3½–4 minutes, depending on how you like your eggs done.
2. Meanwhile, cook the asparagus tips in a frying pan of boiling salted water for 3–4 minutes until tender but still a little crunchy.
3. Drain the eggs and place in egg-cups. Break away the tops of the eggs and add a little butter and seasoning to each yolk. Use the asparagus like 'soldiers' for dipping and serve with wholemeal bread or toast.

FRIED HALLOUMI CHEESE WITH EGGS

This is a Middle Eastern dish which lends itself to all sorts of cheeses. Gouda, Cheddar and Gruyère will work equally well.

1 tablespoon flour
salt and freshly ground black pepper
2 thin 45g/1½oz slices Halloumi cheese
1 teaspoon each softened butter and olive oil
2 large eggs
1 large or 2 small slices of toast

To serve:
olive oil
½ teaspoon chopped fresh mint or dash of Tabasco sauce

1. Mix the flour with some salt and pepper, then dip the slices of cheese in it so that they are evenly coated on both sides.
2. Heat the butter and oil in a medium-sized frying pan. Add the cheese and fry over a medium-high heat for 1 minute on each side until golden brown.
3. Push the cheese to one side and lower the heat slightly. Break in the eggs and fry until the whites are set and the yolks are to your liking.
4. Place the cheese slices on the toasted bread, then top with the fried eggs. Drizzle with a little olive oil, season to taste and sprinkle with the chopped mint or a dash of Tabasco.

FRENCH OMELETTE

2 large eggs
salt and freshly ground black pepper
1 teaspoon cold water
15g/½oz butter

1. Break the eggs into a bowl, season with salt and pepper, and add the water. Beat together lightly with a fork.
2. Melt the butter in a 15cm/6 inch non-stick or heavy-based frying pan, swirling it around so that it coats the sides of the pan.
3. When the butter is foaming, pour in the eggs and cook over a medium-high heat, drawing in the set egg from the sides of the pan and allowing the liquid egg to run underneath.
4. As soon as the omelette is set underneath but still slightly creamy on top, flip one half over the other, slide out on to a warm plate and serve.

VARIATIONS

Buttery herb omelette: Stir a little extra melted butter and 1 tablespoon finely chopped fresh herbs, such as parsley, chervil and chives, into the eggs before cooking.

Parmesan and basil omelette: Stir 1 tablespoon finely grated Parmesan cheese and 1 tablespoon finely shredded fresh basil leaves into the eggs before cooking.

Bacon and croûton omelette: Slice the crusts off a 1cm/½ inch-thick slice of white bread. Cut the remaining bread into 1cm/½ inch cubes. Heat 1 tablespoon sunflower oil in a 15cm/6 inch frying pan. Add the cubes of bread and fry over a medium-high heat for 1½–2 minutes until golden. Set aside on absorbent paper. Heat another 2 teaspoons oil in the frying pan, add 3 chopped rashers rindless back bacon and fry for 2 minutes. Drain on absorbent paper, then mix with the croûtons. Wipe out the pan with absorbent paper, then make the omelette as described above until lightly set on top. Sprinkle the croûton mixture and 30g/1oz grated Cheddar cheese over one half. Flip over the other half and slide on to a warm plate. Sprinkle with chopped parsley before serving.

THAI CRAB OMELETTE

Crab is only available in 110g/4oz cans, but this omelette is so good it is worth making and using the leftover crab in a salad or sandwich the next day.

56ml/2 fl oz chicken stock (see page 162)
¾ teaspoon fish sauce or dark soy sauce (see page 15)
½ teaspoon soft, light brown sugar
¼ teaspoon sesame oil
2 large eggs
salt and freshly ground black pepper
2 teaspoons sunflower oil
½ teaspoon freshly grated ginger root
30g/1oz mangetout, finely shredded
55g/2oz canned white crabmeat, drained
30g/1oz fresh beansprouts
small bunch fresh chives, cut into 2.5cm/1 inch pieces

1. Put the stock, ½ teaspoon of the fish sauce, a pinch of the soft brown sugar and the sesame oil into a small pan, bring to the boil and simmer very gently for 1 minute. Keep hot over a very low heat.
2. Break the eggs into a bowl, add the rest of the fish sauce, sugar and some salt and pepper and beat together lightly. Set aside.
3. Heat 1 teaspoon of the sunflower oil in a small saucepan over a high heat. Add the ginger and mangetout and stir-fry for 1 minute. Add the crabmeat and beansprouts and stir-fry for 1 minute.

Add almost all the chives and leave over a low heat.
4. Heat the remaining oil in a 15cm/6 inch heavy-based or non-stick frying pan. Pour in the egg mixture and cook over a medium-high heat, pulling the cooked egg to the centre of the pan and allowing the liquid egg from the middle to run underneath. Tilt the pan to help the process. Cook until the omelette is set underneath but still slightly creamy on top.
5. Spoon the crab mixture on to one half of the omelette, flip over the other half and slide on to a warm plate. Pour over the sauce and serve garnished with the remaining chives.

TORTILLA

Spanish *tortillas* have no connection with the Mexican variety, apart from sharing a name, which means a round cake. The classic Spanish recipe given here is a thick omelette made with potato and served as a snack or *tapas*. It also makes a speedy supper served hot or cold with crusty bread and salad.

SERVES 2
1 waxy potato weighing about 170g/6oz
2 tablespoons olive oil
3 large eggs
salt and freshly ground black pepper

1. Peel the potato and cut into 1cm/½ inch cubes. Heat half the olive oil in a heavy-based frying pan about 15cm/6 inches in diameter. Add the potatoes, then cover and cook gently for about 15 minutes until the potatoes are tender.
2. Meanwhile, beat the eggs together in a mixing bowl and season with salt and pepper.
3. When the potatoes are cooked, tip them into the egg mixture. Wipe out the pan with absorbent paper. Add the remaining tablespoon of oil and heat. Return the egg mixture to the pan and cook gently until firm and golden brown underneath and round the edges. The tortilla will still be runny in the middle.
4. Place a plate over the frying pan, hold together firmly, then turn over so that the tortilla is transferred to the plate. Slide the tortilla, runny side down, back into the pan and continue to cook until set underneath.

BRUNCH TORTILLA

This is a variation on the classic *tortilla* for those occasions when hunger strikes mid-morning. Serve with warm fresh bread and good strong coffee.

1 good-quality, meaty sausage
1 teaspoon sunflower oil
2 rashers rindless back bacon
15g/½ oz butter
4 button mushrooms, halved
2 large eggs
salt and freshly ground black pepper
1 tomato, skinned

1. Twist the sausage in half, then cut each half lengthways into quarters. Heat the oil in a 15cm/6 inch frying pan. Add the sausage pieces to the pan and fry gently for 1 minute on each side until well browned. Set aside on a plate.
2. Add the bacon to the pan and fry for 1 minute on each side. Set aside with the sausage pieces.
3. Add the butter to the pan, and when melted add the mushrooms and fry for 1 minute, stirring. Return the sausage and bacon to the pan.
4. Beat the eggs with a little salt and pepper. (Go easy on the salt because the bacon and sausages are already quite salty.) Pour into the pan and cook over a low heat for 10 minutes or until set. Heat the grill to high.
5. Cut the skinned tomato into 6 wedges and season to taste. Scatter over the top of the tortilla and grill for 2–3 minutes until the tomatoes are cooked and the tortilla has lightly browned.

FETA FRITTATA

A *frittata* is a flat, *tortilla*-like omelette which can be made with all sorts of savoury ingredients as well as, or instead of, the potato. This is a good brunch dish served with lemon and thyme-baked potatoes (see page 148), crusty bread or salad.

SERVES 1–2
3 large eggs, beaten
salt and freshly ground black pepper
1 tablespoon olive oil
55g/2oz feta cheese, crumbled
6 green olives, halved (optional)

1. Season the eggs with salt and pepper. Heat the olive oil in a heavy-based frying pan about 15cm/6 inches in diameter. Tip in the egg mixture and cook gently until set underneath and round the edges.
2. Crumble the feta into the runny centre, add the olives and continue to cook gently until the base and sides are firm.
3. Place a plate over the frying pan, hold together firmly, then turn over so that the *frittata* is now on the plate. Slide the *frittata*, runny side down, back into the pan and continue to cook until set underneath. Serve hot or cold.

SCRAMBLED EGGS

2 large eggs
salt and freshly ground black pepper
15g/½oz butter
1 tablespoon double cream (optional)

To serve:
wholemeal toast

Break the eggs into a bowl and season with salt and pepper. Beat together lightly with a fork. Melt half the butter in a small, non-stick pan. Swirl it around the pan so that it coats the sides a little, then add the eggs and cook over a medium heat, stirring all the time, for about 2 minutes or until the eggs are half set. Take off the heat, add the remaining butter and the cream (if using), and keep stirring, returning to the heat briefly if necessary, until the eggs are soft and creamy. Serve with wholemeal toast.

VARIATIONS

Scrambled eggs with Boursin: Stir 20g/¾oz Boursin or another herb and garlic flavoured cream cheese into the half-cooked eggs with the remaining butter and continue cooking until soft and creamy.

Scrambled eggs with smoked salmon: Arrange 45g/1½oz thinly sliced smoked salmon on a plate. Make the scrambled eggs with the double cream. Stir 1 teaspoon chopped fresh chives or dill into the eggs at the end of cooking and serve with the smoked salmon.

Scrambled eggs with anchovies: Drain 4 small anchovy fillets on absorbent paper for a minute or two. Chop into small pieces and stir into the eggs towards the end of cooking.

Devilled eggs with mushrooms: Beat the eggs with ¼ teaspoon Dijon mustard, 2 dashes Worcestershire sauce and 2 drops Tabasco sauce. Melt 15g/½oz butter in a pan. Add 55g/2oz roughly chopped button mushrooms and stir-fry for 30 seconds. Add the eggs to the pan and cook, stirring until half set. Take off the heat, stir in 1 tablespoon double cream, the remaining butter and 1 teaspoon chopped fresh parsley and continue cooking until soft and creamy.

Scrambled eggs with grilled asparagus: Trim the bottom of 5 medium–thick asparagus spears by taking hold of the stalk towards the end and bending it until it snaps – this will get rid of the inedible, woody part. Heat the grill to medium. Lay the spears on the rack of the grill pan, brush with melted butter mixed with a little olive oil and grill for about 7 minutes, turning and brushing with more butter and oil halfway through cooking. Meanwhile, cook the scrambled eggs, stirring in 1 teaspoon chopped fresh chervil or parsley at the end of cooking. Serve the asparagus with the scrambled eggs, sprinkled with freshly grated Parmesan cheese, and toasted French bread drizzled with the buttery juices from the grill pan.

INDIAN SCRAMBLED EGGS

15g/½oz butter
½ small onion, very finely chopped
1cm/½ inch fresh ginger, peeled and
finely grated
½ small, fresh green chilli, seeded and
very finely chopped (see page 15)
pinch ground turmeric
¼ teaspoon ground cumin
1 tomato, skinned, seeded and chopped
2 large eggs
salt and cayenne pepper
1 teaspoon chopped fresh coriander

To serve:
naan bread

1. Melt the butter in a small pan. Add the onion and cook gently for 5 minutes until soft. Add the ginger and chilli and fry for 1 minute. Add the turmeric, cumin and tomato and fry for 1 minute.
2. Beat the eggs with salt and cayenne pepper. Add to the pan and cook, stirring, over a medium heat until the eggs are soft and creamy. Stir in the coriander and serve with warm buttered naan bread.

EGGS IN COCONUT CURRY SAUCE

1 tablespoon sunflower oil
1 small onion, thinly sliced
1 garlic clove, crushed
1cm/½ inch piece fresh ginger root,
finely grated
2 teaspoons ground almonds
¼ teaspoon cayenne pepper
¼ teaspoon ground turmeric
½ teaspoon ground coriander
½ teaspoon ground cumin
½ teaspoon finely chopped red chilli
(see page 15)
200g/7oz can chopped tomatoes
1 small bay leaf or 2 curry leaves
15g/½oz creamed coconut
salt
2 large eggs, hardboiled

For the garnish:
1 tablespoon natural yoghurt
chopped fresh coriander

To serve:
naan bread or basmati rice (see page 70)

1. Heat the oil in a saucepan. Add the onion and fry over a medium-high heat for 5 minutes. Add the garlic and fry for another minute until both are well browned.
2. Meanwhile, put the ginger, almonds, cayenne pepper, turmeric, coriander and cumin into a bowl and add enough cold water to make a smooth paste.
3. Reduce the heat under the onions and add the chilli. Cook for 30 seconds. Add the spice paste and fry gently for 2 minutes.
4. Add the chopped tomatoes and bay or curry leaves. Dissolve the creamed coconut in 56ml/2 fl oz boiling water. Add to the pan, season with salt to taste and simmer for 15 minutes. Remove the bay leaf or curry leaves.
5. Shell and halve the hardboiled eggs. Add them to the pan, spoon a little sauce over each egg and simmer for 3–4 minutes or until the eggs are hot. Garnish with the yoghurt and chopped coriander and serve with either basmati rice or warm naan bread.

SWISS BAKED EGGS

1 large slice cooked ham
1 large slice white bread, 1cm/½ inch
thick
1 tablespoon Kirsch, dry white wine or
milk
2 large eggs
salt and freshly ground black pepper
55g/2oz Gruyère cheese, coarsely grated

1. Heat the oven to 180°C/350°F/gas
mark 4. Lay the slice of ham in the
bottom of an oiled gratin dish so that it
comes up the sides a little. Lay the bread
on top and sprinkle with the Kirsch,
wine or milk.
2. Break the eggs on top of the bread,
season to taste, then sprinkle with the
cheese. Bake at the top of the oven for
12–15 minutes until golden.

PASTA & RICE

PASTA AND RICE

There is little doubt that pasta and rice are two of the most useful and versatile ingredients in the store cupboard.

PASTA

This is almost certainly the perfect one-person supper: quick to prepare, available in a multitude of shapes and forms, and delicious with an infinite number of accompaniments.

It is made from hard durum wheat, so as to absorb only the minimum amount of water when it cooks, but should be cooked in plenty of boiling, salted water to avoid it sticking together. Make sure the water is at a rolling boil before adding the pasta, then stir occasionally to make sure it stays separate. Adding a few drops of olive oil to the cooking water to help separation is a matter of personal preference. Cook dried pasta for approximately 10 minutes, and fresh pasta for 3 minutes. Test for readiness by tasting a piece: it should still have a slight firmness or bite. Pasta al dente, as it is known, mixes perfectly with sauces and dressings, but overcooked pasta tends to become a sticky mass.

It doesn't especially matter what shape or type of pasta is chosen for any particular dish. Generally, long thin pasta is served with simple sauces of tomato, butter, oil, herbs, garlic or cheese. The richer, more complex sauces cling better to shaped pasta, such as butterflies, bows or rigatoni, where the sauce can fill the hollows and curves.

The recipes in this section allow 110g/4oz of pasta as an average portion but this amount can be adjusted to suit individual appetites.

The excellent varieties of fresh, filled pasta available from supermarkets make a meal in a moment. They can simply be tossed with butter and grated Parmesan or any of the quick pasta sauces described below. To complete the meal, serve the pasta with a green salad, a tomato salad or an avocado, tomato and mozzarella salad (see pages 149 and 150), plus olives, grissini (breadsticks), sliced salami or Parma ham. A full-bodied red wine is a must.

All recipes serve 1 unless stated otherwise.

QUICK PASTA SAUCES

Each of the following recipes makes enough for one.

BUTTER AND GARLIC SAUCE
30g/1oz butter
1 garlic clove, crushed
1 tablespoon chopped parsley
1 tablespoon grated Parmesan cheese

Melt the butter, add the garlic and cook for 1 minute. Stir in the cooked pasta and toss together with the parsley and Parmesan.

WALNUT 'PESTO' SAUCE
30g/1oz butter
1 garlic clove, chopped
4 walnuts, chopped
salt and freshly ground black pepper
1 tablespoon chopped parsley

Melt the butter. Add the garlic and chopped walnuts and fry for 1 minute. Add the cooked pasta, season with salt and plenty of ground black pepper, toss together until evenly coated and serve sprinkled with parsley.

LEMON AND HERB SAUCE
grated zest from ½ lemon
1 tablespoon chopped assorted fresh herbs
1 tablespoon olive oil

Mix the zest, herbs and oil together. Drain the pasta, return to the pan. Pour in the oil mixture and toss well.

CARBONARA
1 teaspoon oil
30g/1oz pancetta or bacon, diced
1 egg
2 tablespoons cream
freshly ground black pepper
1 tablespoon Parmesan cheese

Heat the oil and fry the pancetta or bacon until slightly browned and the fat has melted. Beat together the egg and cream. Drain the pasta and add to the pan with the bacon. Pour in the egg and cream mixture, stirring quickly. Season with ground black pepper, add the Parmesan and stir again. Serve immediately.

CHILLED TOMATO SAUCE
1 beefsteak tomato, peeled and deseeded
1 garlic clove
1 spring onion, chopped
1 teaspoon chopped fresh basil
2 tablespoons olive oil
salt and freshly ground black pepper

Chop the tomato flesh finely. Flatten the garlic with the back of a knife. Mix all the ingredients together and season. Cover and chill for 3–4 hours or overnight. Remove the garlic and serve the sauce on top of piping hot, freshly cooked pasta.

PASTA WITH LEMON PRAWN AND DILL SAUCE

110g/4oz green tagliatelle
75ml/3 fl oz double cream
grated zest and juice of ½ lemon
110g/4oz frozen prawns, defrosted
1 tablespoon fresh chopped dill
salt and freshly ground black pepper

To serve:
grated Parmesan cheese

1. Cook the tagliatelle in plenty of boiling salted water.
2. Put the cream and lemon zest into a small, heavy-based pan. Bring to the boil and simmer for 2 minutes. Stir in the lemon juice, prawns, dill and seasoning.
3. Drain the tagliatelle. Return to the pan and stir in the sauce. Serve on a warm plate and sprinkle sparingly with Parmesan cheese.

TAGLIATELLE WITH SPINACH, PINENUTS AND RAISINS

110g/4oz tagliatelle
110g/4oz fresh baby spinach
1 tablespoon olive oil
30g/1oz pinenuts
30g/1oz raisins
salt and freshly ground black pepper
freshly grated nutmeg
15g/½ oz butter
1 garlic clove, crushed

To serve:
shavings of Parmesan cheese

1. Cook the tagliatelle in plenty of boiling salted water.
2. Remove any tough stalks from the spinach. Wash well and dry with absorbent paper or a clean tea towel. Heat the oil in a large, heavy-based frying pan. Add the pinenuts and raisins and fry briefly. Add the spinach and toss over the heat until wilted. Season with salt, plenty of ground black pepper and nutmeg.
3. Drain the pasta. Melt the butter in the pan and add the garlic. Fry gently for 1 minute. Return the tagliatelle to the pan and stir until evenly coated with the garlic butter. Serve on a warm plate. Spoon the spinach mixture on top and scatter with shavings of Parmesan.

VARIATION
Substitute the raisins with 55g/2oz diced pancetta. .

PASTA WITH FRESH AUBERGINE SAUCE

1 tablespoon olive oil
1 small red onion, peeled and sliced
1–2 garlic cloves, crushed
pinch ground cumin
¼ medium-sized aubergine, diced
110g/4oz pasta shapes
1 ripe beefsteak or large tomato, peeled and diced
salt and freshly ground black pepper
extra olive oil
few fresh basil leaves

1. Heat the olive oil in a heavy-based pan and fry the onion until softened. Add the garlic and cumin and fry for 1 minute. Stir in the aubergine and cook gently until soft and starting to brown.
2. Meanwhile, cook the pasta in plenty of boiling salted water.
3. Add the tomato to the sauce and season with salt and pepper. Stir well and leave over a low heat.
4. Drain the pasta and return to the pan. Moisten with a little olive oil then stir in the aubergine sauce. Top with torn basil leaves.

SPAGHETTI WITH MUSSELS

This is a version of *Spaghetti con vongole* made with mussels, as fresh clams can prove difficult to find.

1 tablespoon olive oil
½ small onion, finely chopped
1 garlic clove, chopped
225g/8oz tin chopped tomatoes
50ml/½ glass red wine
good pinch dried basil
salt and freshly ground black pepper
110g/4oz spaghetti
225g/8oz fresh mussels
chopped parsley

1. Heat the oil in a heavy-based pan. Add the onion and fry gently until soft and transparent. Stir in the garlic and cook for a further minute. Add the tomatoes, wine, basil and seasoning. Simmer for 20–30 minutes until well reduced.
2. Cook the spaghetti in a large pan of boiling salted water.
3. Scrub the mussels well and pull away the 'beard' (seaweed-like threads). Tap the mussels on the worktop and discard any that stay open or feel heavy for their size. Put the mussels into the pan with the tomato sauce. Cover and cook gently for about 5 minutes until the mussels have opened. Discard any that stay closed.
4. Drain the spaghetti and pile on to a warm plate. Spoon the sauce on top and sprinkle with parsley.

PASTA WITH SICILIAN SAUCE

SERVES 2
1 fennel bulb
1 tablespoon olive oil
½ medium onion, chopped
1 garlic clove, crushed
225g/8oz tin chopped tomatoes
½ teaspoon tomato purée
2 tablespoons red wine
30g/1oz sultanas
salt and freshly ground black pepper
pinch caster sugar
110g/4oz pasta shapes

To serve:
chopped fennel tops or flat-leaf parsley
shavings of Parmesan cheese

1. Remove the outer layer of the fennel bulb, saving the feathery green tops. Roughly chop.
2. Heat the oil in a heavy-based pan and fry the onion and fennel gently until soft and transparent. Add the crushed garlic and fry for 1 minute. Stir in the chopped tomatoes, tomato purée, wine and sultanas. Season with salt, pepper and the sugar. Simmer for 30–40 minutes until reduced to a rich sauce.
3. Boil the pasta in plenty of boiling water, then drain and return to the pan. Stir in the sauce and serve topped with the chopped herbs and shavings of Parmesan.

NOODLES WITH CHILLI PRAWNS AND CUCUMBER

2 teaspoons peanut butter, crunchy or smooth
30g/1oz creamed coconut, chopped
2 tablespoons boiling water
salt and freshly ground black pepper
85g/3oz rice or egg noodles
110g/4oz large, shelled prawns, defrosted if frozen
1 teaspoon sesame oil
1 red chilli, deseeded and chopped (see page 15)
1 teaspoon peeled and finely chopped fresh ginger
2 spring onions, cleaned and chopped
30g/1oz peanuts
1 tablespoon diced cucumber

1. Mix the peanut butter, creamed coconut and boiling water together to make a smooth paste. Add a large pinch of salt.
2. Cook the noodles in plenty of boiling salted water.
3. Meanwhile, with a sharp knife, remove the black vein from the back of the prawns.
4. Heat the sesame oil in a heavy-based frying pan or wok. Add the chilli, ginger, spring onion and peanuts and fry for 1 minute. Add the prawns. Season with salt and pepper and toss over a brisk heat for a further 2 minutes.
5. Drain the noodles. Return to the pan and stir in the peanut butter mixture. Serve topped with the chilli prawns and diced cucumber.

PASTA WITH SUN-DRIED TOMATOES AND SOFT CHEESE

110g/4oz tagliatelle
1 tablespoon olive oil
2 sun-dried tomatoes, chopped, or 1
teaspoon red pesto
1 garlic clove, chopped
55g/2oz soft cheese, such as mild goat's
cheese, Boursin or ricotta
freshly ground black pepper
chopped parsley

1. Boil the pasta in plenty of salted
water.
2. Mix together the olive oil, tomatoes
or pesto and garlic.
3. Drain the pasta. Add the olive oil
mixture to the pan and stir over the heat
for 1 minute. Return the pasta to the
pan. Add the cheese in small spoonfuls.
Season with plenty of ground black
pepper, give a final stir and serve
immediately sprinkled with chopped
parsley.

PASTA FLORENTINE

55g/2oz pasta shapes
15g/½oz butter
1 garlic clove, peeled
1 tomato, peeled and sliced
110g/4oz frozen spinach, defrosted
salt and freshly ground black pepper
freshly grated nutmeg
150ml/¼ pint cheese sauce (see page 159)
2 tablespoons double cream
1 tablespoon grated Parmesan cheese

1. Cook the pasta in plenty of boiling
salted water, then drain well. Preheat
the oven to 190°C/375°F/gas mark 5.
2. Meanwhile, melt the butter in a pan
and when foaming, add the garlic and
tomato and fry briefly on both sides.
Lift into the base of a small, ovenproof
dish.
3. Add the spinach and cook in the same
pan until all the moisture has
evaporated. Season with salt, pepper
and nutmeg. Spoon the spinach on top
of the tomato.
4. Make the cheese sauce, add the cream
and stir into the cooked pasta. Season to
taste and spoon the spinach on top.
Sprinkle with Parmesan cheese. Bake
for 15–20 minutes until golden brown
and bubbling.

LASAGNE

*¼ quantity bolognese sauce (see
page 122)
2 sheets no-cook lasagne
150ml/¼ pint cheese sauce (see page 159)
85g/3oz mozzarella cheese, sliced*

1. Set the oven to 190°C/375°F/gas
mark 5. Lay a sheet of lasagne at the
bottom of a small, ovenproof dish.
Cover with half the meat sauce. Top
with a second layer of pasta and meat
sauce.
2. Pour the cheese sauce over the meat.
Arrange the sliced mozzarella on top.
Bake for 40 minutes until bubbling and
browned.

VARIATION

For a vegetable lasagne, substitute the
bolognese sauce with a ½ quantity of
ratatouille with chick peas (see
page 136).

GRILLED VEGETABLE TOPPING FOR PASTA OR COUSCOUS

Any leftovers of this delicious topping may be served as a salad or side dish to accompany another meal. The vegetables are very good with grilled fish or meat.

SERVES 2
1 small aubergine
1 courgette
1 red or yellow pepper
½ small red onion, peeled
3 tablespoons olive oil
salt and freshly ground black pepper
12 fresh basil leaves
1 teaspoon balsamic vinegar
110g/4oz short pasta or 30g/1oz
couscous per person
15g/½ oz butter
1 garlic clove, crushed

1. Heat the grill to its highest temperature. Slice the aubergine into 0.5cm/¼ inch circles and slice the courgette diagonally. Remove the stalk and seeds from the pepper and cut into four. Cut the red onion into four wedges.
2. Brush the vegetables liberally with olive oil and grill until dark brown and charred. The peppers will quickly turn almost black, so remove them. Turn the remaining vegetables, brush with oil and grill until brown.
3. Peel the skin from the peppers and cut the flesh into strips. Cut the aubergine slices in half. Layer the vegetables in a small dish, sprinkling each layer with salt, pepper, basil leaves and balsamic vinegar. Leave to cool.
4. Cook the pasta in plenty of boiling salted water. Drain.
5. Melt the butter in the pan, add the garlic and cook for 1 minute. Add the pasta and stir until evenly coated in the garlic butter. Alternatively, if using couscous, prepare according to the instructions on page 73 and fork in the garlic and butter. Top with the cooled, grilled vegetables.

RICE

There are thousands of kinds of rice, but just a few of them are of particular interest to cooks:
Basmati rice is long-grained and has a unique nutty flavour. It is less inclined to become sticky than other long-grain rices.
Thai fragrant rice is another good all-rounder. It is a little stickier than basmati, but has a wonderful scented flavour. It is particularly good for serving with Southeast Asian food.
Wild rice has black grains and is really an aquatic grass. If cooked alone, the flavour, along with the price, can be overpowering. It is a good idea to dilute both by adding a small handful of it to

basmati rice.

Brown rice has been hulled but not lost its bran, so it is more nutritious and filling than white rice but has a much heavier texture. Brown rice takes about 45 minutes to cook.

Arborio and **carnaroli** are two top-grade risotto rices. The plump, round grains are able to absorb large amounts of liquid without becoming mushy. Both are available from supermarkets.

All recipes serve 1 unless stated otherwise.

BASMATI RICE

This is an excellent method of cooking rice, which consistently produces dry, separate grains. It also allows both flavour and timing to be flexible. This method works well with any long-grain rice, except brown, which takes too long to cook.

15g/½oz butter or oil
55g/2oz basmati rice
150ml/¼ pint water or stock (see page 162–163)
salt and ground black pepper

1. Melt the butter in a small, heavy-based pan. Add the rice and fry gently for a minute or two until it is well coated.
2. Pour in the water or stock. Take care as it may hiss and splutter. Season with salt and ground black pepper and boil vigorously until little craters appear on the surface. Remove from the heat, cover with a piece of foil and a tight-fitting lid and leave to stand for 15 minutes.

VARIATIONS
- Gently fry 1 tablespoon finely chopped onion before frying the rice.
- Add a small pinch of turmeric to the rice when frying.
- Add a pinch of saffron with the seasoning.
- Gently fry 1 tablespoon finely chopped onion, then add a pinch of ground turmeric, cumin, cinnamon and mixed spice and fry with the rice; add a few sultanas with the liquid.
- Add a small handful of wild rice to the basic ingredients.

NOTE: The rice can stand for up to half an hour without spoiling and will still be hot. If left longer, it will reheat well in a microwave oven.

FLAT MUSHROOM RISOTTO

225g/8oz flat mushrooms
55g/2oz butter
½ medium onion, finely chopped
55g/2oz arborio or carnaroli rice
salt and freshly ground black pepper
150ml/¼ pint warm white wine or
vegetable stock (see page 163)
1 tablespoon grated or shaved Parmesan
cheese

1. Roughly chop the mushrooms. Melt the butter, add the onion and fry gently until soft and transparent. Add the mushrooms and continue to fry for a further 10 minutes.
2. Add the rice and stir until coated with butter. Season with 1 teaspoonful salt and some freshly ground black pepper. Gradually stir in the wine or stock, allowing each addition to become absorbed before adding more. This will take about 15 minutes.
3. Spoon the rice on to a warm plate and serve topped with Parmesan cheese.

NOTE: Using wine rather than stock gives this dish a deliciously alcoholic flavour.

BLUE CHEESE RISOTTO

30g/1oz butter
1 garlic clove, chopped
55g/2oz arborio or carnaroli rice
290ml/½ pint warm chicken or
vegetable stock (see page 162–163) or
half and half with white wine
salt and freshly ground black pepper
1 tablespoon double cream
30g/1oz Dolcelatte, Gorgonzola or
Roquefort cheese
2 tablespoons grated Parmesan cheese
1 teaspoon torn basil leaves

To serve:
whole basil leaves
shaved Parmesan cheese

1. Melt the butter in a heavy-based sauté pan. Add the garlic and fry gently until golden brown. Stir in the rice and fry until well covered in the garlic butter.
2. Gradually stir in the stock, allowing each addition to become absorbed before adding more. This will take about 15 minutes. The risotto should have a creamy, 'rice pudding' texture.
3. Season with salt and pepper. Stir in the cream and crumble in the blue cheese. Add the Parmesan and torn basil. Give a quick stir before serving. Top with basil leaves and extra Parmesan.

BROWN RICE WITH SPICED CHICKEN, TOMATO AND COURGETTE

A cross between a pilaff and a stir-fry, this recipe is ideal served with a green salad.

1 tablespoon oil
½ onion, finely chopped
55g/2oz brown rice
290ml/½ pint chicken stock (see page 162)
salt and freshly ground black pepper
1 courgette
1 tomato, peeled and deseeded
1 chicken breast fillet
1 level teaspoon Cajun spice (see page 80)
15g/½oz butter
lemon juice
chopped parsley

1. Heat half the oil in a saucepan. Fry the onion gently until soft and transparent. Add the rice and continue to fry until well coated with oil. Pour in the stock and seasoning. Bring to the boil and simmer gently for 40–50 minutes, until the rice is tender. Stir occasionally.
2. Trim the courgette and cut into 1cm/ ½ inch chunks. Cut the tomato into similar-sized pieces. Cut the chicken breast into strips and then into 2.5cm/1 inch pieces. Dust lightly with the Cajun spice.

3. When the rice is nearly cooked heat the remaining oil in a heavy-based frying pan. Add the butter and when foaming, fry the chicken briskly until well browned. Add the courgette and tomato and toss over the heat for a few minutes until the courgette is hot but still crunchy and the chicken cooked.
4. Add the cooked rice to the pan with the chicken. Check the seasoning, then add the lemon juice and sprinkle with chopped parsley.

COUSCOUS

Couscous is made from flour-coated grains of semolina and is used in cooking throughout North Africa and the Middle East. It is simple to prepare and an interesting alternative to rice as an accompaniment to any main course. Traditionally, it is served with robust meat or vegetable stews, such as Italian lamb casserole (see page 125) or ratatouille with chick peas (see page 136), but is equally good with marinated chicken or lamb. Couscous is often served with a hot chilli sauce called *harissa*, but it may also be served plain or with a flavoured butter.

30g/1oz couscous
56ml/2 fl oz water, chicken or vegetable stock (see page 162–163)

1. Cover the couscous with the water or stock and leave to stand for 10 minutes.
2. Line a sieve or small steamer with muslin or a clean j-cloth. Spoon in the couscous and steam over water or a simmering stew for 20 minutes. Alternatively, microwave on full power for 2 minutes. Fluff up with a fork before serving.

VARIATIONS
- Fork in a knob of savoury butter flavoured with chilli and coriander, cumin or garlic (see page 165).
- Stir in 1 tablespoon mixed chopped nuts and dried apricots.

FISH

FISH

A tender, flaky fillet of fish requires little cooking, and as fish is high in protein and low in fat, it is an ideal choice for health-conscious lone cooks. It is best to buy fish on the day it is to be cooked. Fishmongers can offer a wide choice and will fillet and trim to your requirements.

There are not too many hard and fast rules when it comes to choosing which fish to cook in what way. Recipes in this section clearly indicate when a particular fish should be used and when a choice can be made. 'White fish' means a firm white fish and can be any of the following: halibut, haddock, cod, hake and turbot or whiting.

All recipes serve 1 unless stated otherwise.

HADDOCK AND CIDER PIE

SERVES 2
110g/4oz haddock
110g/4oz smoked haddock
150ml/¼ pint milk
2 hardboiled eggs
20g/¾oz butter
20g/¾oz flour
150ml/¼ pint cider or apple juice
1 tablespoon chopped parsley
salt and freshly ground black pepper
lemon juice
2 quantities mashed potato with spring onions (see page 146)

1. Set the oven to 190°C/375°F/gas mark 5. Wash the fish and place skin side up in an ovenproof dish. Pour in the milk, then cover and bake for about 15 minutes until opaque and firm to touch.

2. Lift out the fish and reserve the liquid. Remove the skin and any bones, then flake the fish into large pieces. Place in a pie dish. Slice the eggs and arrange on top of the fish.

3. Melt the butter in a saucepan, add the flour and stir for 1 minute. Gradually add the reserved liquid and cider, stirring continuously until the mixture boils and thickens. Stir in the parsley, seasoning and a squeeze of lemon juice. Pour the sauce over the fish and egg.

4. Reset the oven to 200°C/400°F/gas mark 6. Spread the mashed potato evenly over the sauce-topped fish and make a pattern with a fork. Place on a baking sheet and bake for 15–20 minutes until the potato is crisp and golden brown.

FISH IN BUTTERED CRUMBS

*1 × 170g/6oz cod or haddock fillet,
skinned
30g/1oz fresh white breadcrumbs
good pinch dried thyme
salt and freshly ground black pepper
30g/1oz butter, melted*

*To serve:
tomato sauce (see page 160) or tartare
sauce (see page 158)*

1. Set the oven to 200°C/400°F/gas
mark 6. Wash the fish and pat dry with
absorbent paper. Mix together the
breadcrumbs and thyme. Season with
salt and pepper.
2. Dip the fish into the melted butter
and then the breadcrumbs. Press well to
ensure a good covering. Lay the fish on
a baking sheet.
3. Bake for 10–15 minutes until the
crumbs are well browned. Serve with
tartare or tomato sauce.

GRILLED SALMON STEAK

*1 × 170g/6oz salmon steak
melted butter
freshly ground black pepper
lemon juice*

*To serve:
quick hollandaise sauce (see page 159)
or tomato salsa or avocado salsa (see
page 161) or avocado, lime or chilli
coriander butter (see page 165) or
tomato and dill sauce (see page 160) or
simply a wedge of lemon*

1. Heat the grill. Brush the salmon steak
and the base of the grill pan with butter.
Season the fish with pepper and lemon
juice. Lay the fish in the grill pan, not
on the wire tray where it might stick.
2. Grill the fish until pale brown. Turn
over and brush with more melted
butter. Season again with pepper and
lemon juice and grill for a further 3
minutes or until cooked. The fish will
feel firm to touch and the flesh will
flake easily. Serve with the pan juices
poured over and one of the suggested
sauces.

SWORDFISH WITH GINGER AND CORIANDER CRUST

1 × 170–225g/6–8oz swordfish steak
15g/½oz melted butter
lemon juice
salt and freshly ground black pepper

For the crust:
1 tablespoon fresh white breadcrumbs
½ fresh red chilli, deseeded and finely chopped (see page 15)
walnut-sized piece of fresh ginger, peeled and finely chopped
1 tablespoon chopped fresh coriander leaves
30g/1oz butter, melted
salt and freshly ground black pepper

1. Wash the swordfish steak and pat dry with absorbent paper. Brush with melted butter and season with lemon juice, salt and pepper. Heat the grill to the highest temperature.
2. Mix together all the ingredients for the crust and season with salt and pepper.
3. Grill the swordfish steaks on both sides until beginning to brown and the fish feels firm to touch.
4. Spread the crust mixture over the swordfish and continue to grill until well browned. Serve straight away.

KIPPER KEDGEREE

1 large kipper fillet
30g/1oz butter
¼ medium onion, finely chopped
1 teaspoon curry powder (see page 166)
1 quantity cooked rice (see page 70)
1 hardboiled egg, peeled and quartered
salt and freshly ground black pepper
lemon juice
1 tablespoon chopped parsley

To serve:
green salad (see page 150)

1. Lay the kipper in a heatproof dish, cover with boiling water and leave to stand for 2 minutes. Remove the skin and any bones from the kipper, then break the flesh into large pieces.
2. Melt the butter in a heavy-based frying pan. When foaming, add the chopped onion and cook gently until soft and transparent. Stir in the curry powder and cook for 1 minute. Add the rice, kipper and hardboiled egg and stir gently over the heat until warmed all the way through.
3. Season with a little salt and plenty of pepper and lemon juice. Stir in the parsley and serve immediately with a green salad.

RED MULLET WITH ORANGE AND CORIANDER

1 red mullet, filleted and pin boned (see page 21)
salt and freshly ground black pepper
1 tablespoon olive oil
15g/½oz butter
juice and grated zest of 1 small orange
1 tablespoon fresh coriander

1. Wash the mullet fillets and pat dry. Season with salt and pepper.
2. Heat the oil in a heavy-based frying pan, add the butter and when foaming fry the fish for 3 minutes on each side.
3. Pour the orange juice and zest into the pan, bring to the boil and reduce until syrupy. Lift the fillets on to a warm plate. Give the sauce a good stir, add the coriander, pour over the fish and serve immediately.

BLACKENED SWORDFISH

'Blackening' is a term used in Cajun cooking and not an excuse for a burnt supper. It refers to the effect of coating in Cajun spices and cooking on a fierce griddle. The food remains moist and tender inside, while the spice coating cooks to a deep reddish-brown, almost black. Serve with mashed potatoes with spring onions, roast peppers and courgettes.

1 × 170g/6oz swordfish steak
1 teaspoon oil
15g/½oz butter
lemon juice

For the Cajun seasoning:
1 tablespoon black peppercorns
1 tablespoon rock salt
1 teaspoon cayenne pepper
1 teaspoon cumin seeds
1 teaspoon coriander seeds
1 teaspoon dried thyme
1 tablespoon paprika pepper

To serve:
2 lemon wedges
mayonnaise (see page 157)

1. Rinse the swordfish steak and pat very dry with absorbent paper.
2. Make the Cajun seasoning by grinding all the ingredients to a powder with a pestle and mortar or in a coffee grinder.
3. Sprinkle the swordfish with a light coating of Cajun seasoning and press well into the flesh. Store the remaining seasoning in an airtight jar.
4. Heat the oil and butter in a heavy-based frying pan. When foaming, add the swordfish and fry briskly for about 3 minutes a side. The spices will cook and turn black and the fish should feel firm. Squeeze some lemon juice over the fish. Serve with the pan juices poured over, and hand the lemon wedges and mayonnaise separately.

MONKFISH AND BACON KEBABS

110g/4oz monkfish
½ green pepper
4 rashers streaky bacon

For the marinade:
1 tablespoon olive oil
½ lemon or lime
salt and freshly ground black pepper

For the garnish:
lemon or lime slices

1. Discard any residue skin from the monkfish, then cut into four pieces. Lay in a small, shallow dish.
2. Make the marinade: put the oil into a bowl. Squeeze the juice from the lemon or lime, then slice the skin and add both to the oil. Season with salt and pepper. Pour over the fish. Cover tightly and leave to marinate for 2–3 hours.
3. Remove the stalk and seeds from the green pepper and cut into four. Roll the bacon up loosely.
4. Just before serving, heat the grill to its highest temperature. Thread the monkfish, bacon and pepper alternately on to a skewer. Brush with some of the marinade.
5. Grill for 3 minutes a side, brushing several times with the marinade. Serve straight away garnished with slices of lemon or lime.

NOTE: For a touch of luxury, serve with quick hollandaise sauce (see page 159).

HAKE WITH PAPRIKA AND RED PEPPER

This is an especially quick and robust fish dish. Serve with a salad and lemon and thyme potatoes (see page 148).

170g/6oz hake fillets, or any other firm
white fish, skinned and pin boned
15g/½oz plain flour
1 teaspoon paprika
1 tablespoon olive oil
knob of butter
½ red pepper, deseeded and sliced
salt and freshly ground black pepper

1. Wash the fish and pat dry on absorbent paper. Cut into 2cm/1 inch cubes.
2. Mix the flour and paprika together. Put the fish into a large sieve or colander and shake the flour mixture over it. Toss the fish in the flour until evenly coated.
3. Heat the oil in a heavy-based frying pan. Add the butter and when sizzling, add the fish cubes and sliced pepper. Sprinkle with salt and pepper. Toss over a brisk heat until the fish is golden brown and feels firm to touch.

SEAFOOD CASSEROLE

SERVES 2
2 tablespoons olive oil
½ medium onion, finely chopped
1 tomato, peeled and chopped
½ red pepper, deseeded and chopped
1 garlic clove, crushed
150ml/¼ pint white wine
150ml/¼ pint fish stock (see page 162)
salt and freshly ground black pepper
110g/4oz squid
110g/4oz cod fillet, skinned
30g/1oz ground almonds
110g/4oz fresh mussels
110g/4oz fresh prawns, or frozen
prawns, defrosted

1. Heat the olive oil and slowly fry the onion, for about 10 minutes until soft and transparent but not at all coloured. Add the tomato and red pepper and fry gently for 5 minutes, then add the garlic and cook for a further minute. Stir in the wine, stock and seasoning. Bring to the boil and simmer for 30 minutes.
2. Clean the squid (see page 21). Cut the body into rings and the tentacles into small pieces. Cut the cod into cubes. When the sauce is cooked add the squid and cod and cook for a further 10 minutes. Stir in the ground almonds.
3. Make sure the mussels are alive by tapping them on the worktop. Discard any that remain closed or seem heavy for their size. Bring the casserole to simmering point and add the mussels and prawns. Cover and cook for 5 minutes. Discard any mussels that stay closed. Serve immediately.

MUSSELS WITH BEER AND PANCETTA

This recipe and its variations make a pleasant change from *moules marinières*. Serve with crusty bread or lemon and thyme baked potatoes (see page 148).

450g/1lb mussels
30g/1oz butter
½ small onion, finely diced
1 celery stick, finely diced
55g/2oz diced pancetta or smoked bacon
150ml/¼ pint light beer
salt and freshly ground black pepper
1 tablespoon chopped parsley
lemon juice

1. Scrub the mussels well and pull away the 'beard' (seaweed-like threads). Tap the mussels on the worktop and discard any that stay open or feel heavy for their size.
2. Melt the butter in a large pan. Fry the onion, celery and pancetta for a few minutes. Add the beer, bring to the boil and boil for 1 minute. Add the mussels, then cover and simmer for about 5 minutes until they have opened. Discard any that stay closed.
3. Season to taste with salt and pepper (be careful with the salt as the pancetta may be salty). Toss in the parsley and a squeeze of lemon juice at the last minute.

VARIATIONS

Mussels with Stilton: This may sound an odd combination but is delicious. Substitute 3 tablespoons wine and 150ml/¼ pint water for the beer, and 30g/1oz crumbled Stilton for the bacon. Follow the recipe, frying the onion and celery alone. When the mussels are cooked, lift them out of the pan and whisk in the Stilton until melted. Pour over the mussels.

Mussels with Lemon Grass: Prepare the mussels in the usual way. Chop 2 stalks lemon grass. Place a large, heavy-based pan over the heat and fry the onion and celery. Throw in the mussels, lemon grass and 150ml/¼ pint water. Sprinkle with a little salt. Shake over the heat for a few minutes until the mussels have opened.

HALIBUT WITH TOMATO AND CHIVES

170g/6oz halibut or any firm white fish,
skinned
150ml/¼ pint creamy milk
salt and freshly ground black pepper
bayleaf
knob of butter
1 level teaspoon flour
1 tomato, peeled and deseeded
1 tablespoon chopped chives
squeeze of lemon juice

1. Put the halibut and milk into a small, shallow pan. Season with salt and pepper and add the bayleaf. Bring to simmering point, lower the heat, cover with a tight-fitting lid and cook for about 5 minutes. The fish will turn opaque and feel firm to touch when cooked.
2. Meanwhile, mix the butter and flour together to form a smooth paste. Cut the tomato into slivers.
3. Remove the fish from the pan and drain on absorbent paper. Discard the skin, then transfer the fish to a warm plate.
4. Remove the bayleaf from the pan and bring the milk to the boil. Whisk in the flour and butter mixture and cook, stirring all the time as the sauce comes to the boil and thickens. Simmer for 30 seconds, then stir in the tomato and chives. Season to taste, add some lemon juice and pour over the fish.

SKATE WINGS WITH GREEN SALSA

225g/8oz skate wing
slice of onion
1 tablespoon wine vinegar

For the green salsa:
1 tablespoon olive oil
pinch cumin seeds
juice ½ lime
1 green chilli, deseeded and finely
chopped (see page 15)
1 tablespoon fresh chopped coriander

1. Put the skate into a shallow pan and cover with water. Add the onion and vinegar and season with salt. Bring to the boil, then cover and simmer for 10 minutes. Remove from the heat and leave to stand for a further 10 minutes.
2. Remove the fish and drain on absorbent paper. Gently scrape away any skin. Place the skate on a warm plate and keep warm.
3. To make the salsa, heat the oil in a small, heavy-based pan and gently fry the cumin seeds until beginning to take on colour. Add the lime juice, chilli and coriander. Allow to bubble up and pour over the skate immediately.

GRILLED COD WITH TAPENADE

1 × 170g/6oz cod fillet or steak, skinned
15g/½oz melted butter
lemon juice
freshly ground black pepper

For the tapenade:
6 black olives, stoned
1 small garlic clove, peeled
1 teaspoon capers
zest and juice of ½ lemon
1 teaspoon anchovy essence
2 tablespoons olive oil
freshly ground black pepper

For the garnish:
basil leaves

1. Wash the cod and pat dry with absorbent paper. Brush with melted butter and season with lemon juice and ground black pepper. Heat the grill to its highest temperature.
2. To make the tapenade, roughly chop the olives and garlic. Place in a food processor or liquidizer with the other tapenade ingredients and blend until smooth. Check the seasoning.
3. Grill the cod until golden brown. Turn over, brush with more melted butter and grill for a further 3 minutes.
4. Spoon the tapenade on to a warmed plate, lay the cod on top and garnish with fresh basil leaves.

SAUTÉD SALMON WITH SPINACH

1 × 170g/6oz salmon fillet
1 tablespoon olive oil
225g/8oz baby spinach
salt and freshly ground black pepper
freshly grated nutmeg

To serve:
1 tablespoon tomato and pepper dressing (see page 164)

1. Wash the salmon and pat dry with absorbent paper. Brush with a little olive oil and set aside.
2. Wash the spinach thoroughly and remove any tough stalks.
3. Heat half the olive oil in a heavy-based or non-stick frying pan. When hot, add the spinach and toss over the heat for 2 minutes. Season well with salt, pepper and nutmeg. Spoon on to a serving plate and keep warm.
4. Heat the remaining oil and when very hot fry the salmon for 2 minutes on each side. Lay the salmon on top of the spinach. Spoon over the tomato and pepper dressing and serve immediately.

VARIATION
Substitute the tomato and pepper dressing with quick hollandaise (see page 159).

SOY-MARINATED TUNA ON SALAD LEAVES

1 × 170g/6oz fresh tuna steak

For the marinade:
1 tablespoon sunflower oil
2 teaspoons light soy sauce
pinch ground ginger
pinch caster sugar
squeeze of lemon juice
freshly ground black pepper

For the salad:
assorted leaves, such as watercress,
curly endive, lettuce, young spinach or
rocket
1 teaspoon hazelnut or walnut oil

1. Wash the tuna steak and pat dry on absorbent paper. With a sharp knife slice the tuna horizontally into three or four wafer-thin slices and arrange in a shallow dish.
2. Mix all the marinade ingredients together and season with ground black pepper. Pour the marinade over the tuna, then cover and marinate for at least 1 hour.
3. Just before serving, wash and dry the salad leaves. Remove any tough stalks. Toss in the nut oil and pile on to a plate.
4. Brush a heavy-based frying pan with oil and heat until smoking. Sear the tuna for 1 minute per side. Set on top of the salad leaves and pour over the pan juices.

BAKED COD WITH LEMON AND OLIVES

1 × 170g/6oz cod steak, skinned
butter for greasing
1 tablespoon olive oil
½ onion, sliced
1 tablespoon stoned black olives
1 large tomato, peeled and deseeded
salt and freshly ground black pepper
1 teaspoon fresh marjoram or a pinch of dried
1 tablespoon lemon juice

1. Set the oven to 190°C/375°F/gas mark 5. Wash the fish and remove any scales. Pat dry. Butter an ovenproof dish.
2. Heat half the oil and fry the onion until soft and transparent. Put in the base of the prepared dish. Set the fish on top.
3. Cut the olives into slivers and coarsely chop the tomato. Scatter over the fish and season with salt, pepper and marjoram. Spoon over the lemon juice and remaining oil. Cover with buttered greaseproof paper and bake for 20–30 minutes until the fish is opaque and firm to touch.

Hot and Sour Soup

Huevos Rancheros

Noodles with Chilli Prawns and Cucumber

Kipper Kedgeree

Seafood Casserole

Soy-marinated Tuna on Salad Leaves

Chicken Breast with Cumin and Mint

Quail Braised with Red Cabbage and Plums

PAN-FRIED MACKEREL WITH LIME

1 small mackerel, filleted (see page 21)
salt and freshly ground black pepper
15g/½oz butter
zest and juice of ½ lime

For the garnish:
chopped parsley
lime wedge

1. Cut the mackerel into two fillets. Wash thoroughly and pat dry with absorbent paper. Sprinkle with salt and pepper.
2. Melt the butter in the frying pan until foaming. Fry the mackerel slowly over a low heat for 5–6 minutes on each side. The skin should be crisp and brown and the flesh feel firm to touch.
3. Pour in the lime juice and zest. Allow to bubble up. Lift the mackerel on to a warm serving plate. Give the juices a good stir to remove any sediment from the bottom of the pan, then pour over the mackerel. Sprinkle with parsley and serve with a lime wedge.

MONKFISH WITH ANCHOVY AND ROASTED PEPPERS

170g/6oz monkfish
butter for greasing
1 small red pepper
1 small yellow pepper
1 shallot, peeled
2 anchovy fillets
30g/1oz softened butter
1 garlic clove, crushed
1 tablespoon chopped parsley
freshly ground black pepper
lemon juice

1. Wash the monkfish, remove any residue skin and pat dry. Butter an ovenproof dish. Set the oven to 190°C/375°F/gas mark 5.
2. Heat the grill to its highest temperature. Cut the peppers into quarters, then remove the stalk, inner membrane and seeds. Grill the peppers, skin side up, until black and blistered. Cool, then scrape off the skin with a small knife.
3. Chop the shallot and anchovy fillets very finely and beat into the softened butter with the garlic and parsley. Season with black pepper and a good squeeze of lemon juice.
4. Spread the butter mixture over the fish and place in the greased dish. Scatter the peppers over the top and bake for 15–20 minutes, until the fish is firm to touch.

PAN-FRIED COD WITH MUSTARD AND DILL CREAM

1 × 170g/6oz cod fillet, skinned
salt and freshly ground black pepper
15g/½oz unsalted butter
¼ onion, finely chopped
3 tablespoons double cream
1 teaspoon Dijon or seed mustard
2 teaspoons chopped fresh dill or ½ teaspoon dried
lemon juice

1. Wash and dry the cod. Season with salt and pepper.
2. Melt the butter in a frying pan and when foaming, add the onion and fry until soft and transparent. Remove from the pan and set aside. Fry the fish for about 3 minutes a side until golden brown and firm to touch. Transfer to a warm plate.
3. Pour the cream into the pan, stirring to remove any sediment from the bottom. Return the onions to the pan. Add the dill and mustard and simmer for 2 minutes, until the mixture has slightly thickened. Season to taste with salt and pepper, add some lemon juice then pour over the fish and serve immediately.

PEPPERED FISH

1 × 170g/6oz white fish fillets, such as cod, haddock, hake or monkfish, skinned
2 teaspoons flour
1 teaspoon crushed dried peppercorns
salt and freshly ground black pepper
1 tablespoon olive oil
1 tablespoon lime juice
1 tablespoon chopped chives
oil and a knob of butter for frying

1. Wash the fish and pat dry with absorbent paper.
2. Mix the flour with the crushed peppercorns and season with salt. Dip the fish into the flour mixture, pressing well to ensure a good coating.
3. Mix together the oil, lime juice and chives. Season with salt and pepper.
4. Heat the oil in a heavy-based or non-stick frying pan. Add the butter and when foaming, fry the fish for about 3 minutes a side until golden brown and firm to touch.
5. Turn up the heat and pour in the lime juice mixture. Allow to bubble up and reduce a little. Transfer the fish to a warmed plate, cover with the sauce and serve immediately.

PAN-FRIED SARDINES

3–4 fresh sardines
1 tablespoon olive oil
lemon juice
ground black pepper

To serve:
lemon wedges
crusty bread
green salad (see page 150) or tomato
salad (see page 150)

1. Clean the sardines: slit along the belly, remove the innards and wash the fish well under running water. Pat dry with absorbent paper.
2. Brush the fish with oil and sprinkle with lemon juice and black pepper.
3. Brush a very heavy-based frying pan with oil and set over a fierce heat. When piping hot, fry the fish briskly for about 2 minutes a side. Arrange on a warm plate with lemon wedges. Serve with crusty bread and a green or tomato salad.

GRILLED MACKEREL FILLETS WITH APPLE AND POTATO SALAD

2 fresh mackerel fillets (see page 21)
lemon juice
salt and freshly ground black pepper

For the apple and potato salad:
55g/2oz cooked new potatoes
½ dessert apple
1 tablespoon soured cream
1 teaspoon horseradish relish
1 heaped teaspoon chopped fresh dill or
a pinch of dried
lemon juice

1. First prepare the apple and potato salad: cut the potato into 1cm/½ inch chunks. Core the apple but leave the skin on. Cut into the same size chunks as the potato. Mix together with the soured cream, horseradish and dill. Season with salt, pepper and lemon juice. Set aside.
2. Remove the wire rack from the grill pan and heat the grill to its highest temperature. Wash and dry the mackerel. Season with lemon juice, salt and pepper.
3. Place the mackerel fillets, skin side down, in the grill pan and cook for 3–4 minutes. The mackerel should feel firm to touch when cooked.
4. Spoon the salad on to a plate and set the mackerel fillets beside it.

SMOKED HADDOCK WITH SWEETCORN

170g/6oz smoked haddock
freshly ground black pepper
150ml/¼ pint milk
15g/½oz butter
15g/½oz flour
pinch dried mustard and cayenne
pepper
45g/1½oz Cheddar cheese, grated
2 tablespoons frozen, sweetcorn kernels
1 tablespoon dried breadcrumbs

1. Set the oven to 190°C/375°F/gas mark 5. Wash the fish and lay it in an ovenproof dish. Season with pepper and pour over the milk. Cover and bake for 15 minutes.
2. Lift out the fish and reserve the liquid. Skin and flake the fish, removing any bones.
3. Melt the butter, stir in the flour, mustard and cayenne pepper and heat for 1 minute. Gradually add the reserved fish liquor, stirring continuously until boiling, smooth and thick.
4. Stir in 30g/1oz of the cheese plus the sweetcorn and fish and reheat. Taste for seasoning; there should be enough salt in the fish, but you may wish to add a little more pepper.
5. Heat the grill to its highest temperature. Pour the fish mixture into an ovenproof dish. Sprinkle the breadcrumbs and the remaining cheese on top. Grill until well browned.

POULTRY

POULTRY

Choose free-range or corn-fed chickens for flavour, and always buy fresh, even if you want portions to store in the freezer. Ready-frozen chicken portions tend to be small and have more fat than fresh chicken. For small joints choose thighs which have a good proportion of moist, tasty meat. Chicken breasts are convenient but cook with care or they can quickly become dry and tasteless. A good trick is to cut the breast into strips so they can be cooked quickly and retain their succulence. All recipes serve 1 unless stated otherwise.

TANDOORI CHICKEN STRIPS

Chicken breasts cut lengthways into strips, marinated and flash-fried or grilled are moist and tender. An infinite variety of quick dinners can be made in this way using assorted marinades and seasonings.

1 chicken breast cut into strips
lengthways
1 tablespoon Greek yoghurt
½ teaspoon tomato purée
1 garlic clove, crushed
pinch ground cumin, coriander and
chilli
1 teaspoon lemon juice
good pinch of salt

To serve:
rice or couscous (see page 69 and 73)
green salad (see page 150)

Turn the chicken strips in the marinade and leave for at least 1 hour. Heat the grill to its highest temperature and grill the chicken, for 5 minutes turning occasionally.

VARIATIONS:

Soy and chilli marinade: Make a quantity of lamb marinade (see page 126). Marinate the chicken for at least 1 hour. Drain. Heat a little olive oil in a heavy-based frying pan. When hot, add the chicken and fry briskly until well browned and tender. Pour the remaining marinade into the pan. Allow to bubble up and reduce until syrupy.

Cajun chicken: Lightly dust the chicken strips with Cajun seasoning (see Blackened Swordfish, page 80). Heat 1 teaspoon oil and 15g/½oz butter. When foaming, add the chicken and fry until dark brown and tender. Add a squeeze of lemon juice and serve with a dollop of mayonnaise.

Citrus marinade: Make a marinade using the juice of ½ lemon or lime or 1 tablespoon orange juice, 1 tablespoon olive oil, pinch ground cumin, 1 teaspoon fresh marjoram or basil, salt and freshly ground black pepper. Marinate the chicken for at least 1 hour. Drain. Heat a little olive oil in a heavy-based frying pan and when hot, fry the chicken briskly until golden brown and tender. Serve with a fresh salsa (see page 161).

TARRAGON CHICKEN

1 boneless chicken breast, skinned
salt and freshly ground black pepper
15g/½oz unsalted butter
1 tablespoon lemon juice
1 tablespoon fresh, chopped tarragon or
1 teaspoon dried
2 tablespoons chicken stock (see
page 162)
2 tablespoons double cream

1. Cut the chicken breast into three long strips. Season with salt and pepper.
2. Melt the butter in a small sauté pan. Brown the chicken on all sides. Add the lemon juice and dried tarragon, if using. Cover with a tight-fitting lid and shake over a low heat for about 5 minutes, or until the chicken is cooked through.
3. Pour the stock into the pan. Bring to the boil and stir to remove any sediment. Stir in the cream and fresh tarragon. Check the seasoning. Simmer for 1 or 2 minutes until the sauce has thickened a little.

CHICKEN AND BROCCOLI CRUMBLE

110g/4oz cooked chicken, skinned
butter for greasing
110g/4oz broccoli florets (about 6)
15g/½oz butter
¼ onion, chopped
2 teaspoons plain flour
150ml/¼ pint chicken stock (see
page 162)
2 tablespoons creamy milk
salt and freshly ground black pepper

For the crumble:
30g/1oz butter
55g/2oz plain flour
1 tablespoon grated Parmesan cheese
pinch cayenne pepper

1. Cut the chicken into bite-sized chunks. Heat the oven to 200°C/400°F/ gas mark 6. Grease a small, ovenproof dish. Make the crumble by rubbing the butter into the flour until the mixture resembles fine breadcrumbs. Stir in the Parmesan and season with salt, black pepper and cayenne.
2. Boil a small pan of salted water and cook the broccoli until tender but retaining some bite. Drain and douse in cold water.
3. Melt the butter in a saucepan and fry the onion until soft and transparent. Stir in the flour and cook for 1 minute. Gradually add the stock, stirring all the time, until smooth and boiling.
4. Stir in the milk, chicken and broccoli. Season with salt and ground black pepper. Bring back to the boil and simmer for 2 minutes. Pile into the ovenproof dish, then scatter the crumble over the top. Bake for 15–20 minutes until the crumble has browned.

CHICKEN AND SWEET POTATO CASSEROLE

2 chicken thighs
85g/3oz mushrooms
1 carrot
1 medium-sized sweet potato weighing
about 200g/7oz
oil for frying
½ medium onion, sliced
1 garlic clove, crushed
150ml/¼ pint chicken stock (see
page 162)
salt and freshly ground black pepper

1. Remove the skin from the chicken.
Cut the mushroom into quarters. Peel
the carrot and sweet potato and cut into
2.5cm/1 inch chunks.
2. Heat the oil in a saucepan and brown
the chicken pieces all over. Set aside.
Add the onion and fry until golden
brown. Stir in the garlic, mushrooms,
carrot and sweet potato. Cover, lower
the heat and 'sweat' the vegetables for 5
minutes.
3. Pour in the stock, stir to remove any
sediment from the bottom of the pan,
bring to the boil and season well.
Return the chicken to the pan, cover
and simmer very gently for 30 minutes.

❋ *Suitable for freezing.*

MARINATED CHICKEN CASSEROLE

2 chicken thighs
salt and freshly ground black pepper
2 teaspoons oil
15g/½oz butter
½ medium onion, chopped
1 garlic clove, crushed
150ml/¼ pint chicken stock (see
page 162)

For the marinade:
2 teaspoons clear honey
zest and juice of ½ lemon
2 tablespoons dry white wine
sprig fresh thyme

To serve:
grilled radicchio (see page 151) or lentils
(see page 151)

1. Rub the chicken with a good pinch of salt and place in a dish.
2. Make the marinade by dissolving the honey in a little boiling water and mixing it with the remaining ingredients. Season with black pepper. Pour the marinade over the chicken, cover and refrigerate for 2–3 hours or overnight.
3. Remove the chicken from the marinade and pat dry with absorbent paper. Heat the oil in a saucepan; when hot, add the butter and heat until foaming. Brown the chicken all over and set aside.
4. Fry the onion until soft and golden brown. Add the garlic and fry for 1 minute. Pour in the marinade and chicken stock. Bring to the boil, stirring to remove any sediment from the bottom of the pan. Return the chicken to the pan, cover and simmer gently for 30 minutes until tender.
5. Transfer the chicken to a warmed serving plate. Boil the liquid until reduced to a syrupy consistency. Check the seasoning, then spoon the sauce over the chicken. Serve with grilled radicchio or lentils.

❄ *Suitable for freezing.*

GRILLED CHICKEN WITH CABBAGE ANCHOIDE

1 boneless chicken breast, skinned
1 tablespoon olive oil
1 thick lemon slice, cut into chunks
1 tablespoonful fresh chopped oregano
or marjoram
salt and freshly ground black pepper

For the cabbage anchoide:
1 teaspoon olive oil
1 garlic clove, peeled and crushed
2 anchovy fillets, finely chopped
110g/4oz white cabbage, finely
shredded
1 teaspoon balsamic vinegar

1. Place the chicken in a shallow dish. Mix together the olive oil, lemon and oregano and season with plenty of salt and pepper. Pour the mixture over the chicken, cover tightly and refrigerate for at least 3 hours.
2. Heat the grill. Meanwhile, make the cabbage anchoide: heat the oil in a saucepan and gently fry the garlic and chopped anchovies for 1 minute. Stir in the cabbage and vinegar and turn in the hot oil. Season with salt and pepper, cover tightly and leave to cook gently over a very low heat while grilling the chicken.
3. Put the chicken under the grill and cook for about 5 minutes a side. Serve immediately with the cabbage anchoide.

CHICKEN BREASTS WITH CRÈME FRAÎCHE AND RED PESTO

1 boneless chicken breast, skinned
15g/½oz unsalted butter
2 tablespoons chicken stock (see
page 162)
salt and freshly ground black pepper
1 tablespoon crème fraîche
1 teaspoon red pesto

For the garnish:
chopped parsley, basil or watercress

1. Cut the chicken into three long strips. Melt the butter in a frying pan and brown the chicken all over. Add the stock and stir to deglaze the bottom of the pan. Season with salt and pepper. Cover with a tight-fitting lid and shake over a low heat for about 5 minutes until tender.
2. Put the chicken on a warm serving plate. Bring the juices to the boil, then whisk in the crème fraîche and red pesto. Check for seasoning, then pour the sauce over the chicken. Garnish with chopped fresh herbs or a sprig of watercress.

CHICKEN BREAST WITH CUMIN AND MINT

15g/½oz sultanas
1 boneless chicken breast
15g/½oz butter
½teaspoon ground cumin
1 garlic clove, crushed
grated zest of ½ orange
salt and freshly ground black pepper
15g/½oz flaked almonds
1 tablespoon orange juice

For the garnish:
freshly chopped mint

To serve:
basmati rice (see page 70) or couscous
(see page 73)

1. Soak the sultanas in boiling water for 10 minutes.
2. Separate the fillet from the chicken breast and slice the rest into two or three long strips about the same size as the fillet.
3. Melt the butter in a frying pan and brown the chicken on all sides.
4. Add the drained sultanas, cumin, garlic and orange zest. Season with salt and pepper. Toss the chicken over the heat for 5 minutes until tender. Add the almonds and fry for a further minute until brown.
5. Stir in the orange juice, allow to bubble up, then scrape any sediment from the bottom of the pan. Serve immediately with a liberal sprinkling of chopped mint and a helping of basmati rice or couscous.

CHICKEN TABOULEH

Tabouleh is a Middle Eastern dish which makes a good light lunch. Serve with a salad and crusty bread to make a more substantial meal.

55g/2oz cracked wheat
110g/4oz cooked chicken
1 ripe tomato, peeled and deseeded
55g/2oz feta cheese, crumbled
2 spring onions, chopped
5cm/2 inch cucumber wedge, diced
½ red pepper, deseeded and diced
1 tablespoon chopped parsley
1 teaspoon chopped mint
1 teaspoon olive oil
1 teaspoon lemon juice
salt and freshly ground black pepper

1. Cover the cracked wheat with cold water and soak for 15 minutes. Drain well, pressing out as much water as possible.
2. Skin the chicken and cut the meat into bite-sized chunks. Cut the tomato into eighths. Mix together with the cracked wheat and all the remaining ingredients, seasoning well with lemon juice, salt and pepper.

SOUTHERN BAKED CHICKEN

2 chicken thighs
55g/2oz self-raising flour
1 tablespoon chopped parsley
1 level teaspoon ground cumin
1 teaspoon grated lemon zest
salt and freshly ground black pepper
1 egg
1 tablespoon milk
55g/2oz dripping or solid vegetable oil

1. Wash the chicken. Set the oven to 200°C/400°F/gas mark 6.
2. Spoon the flour into a shallow dish or plate and mix in the chopped parsley, cumin and lemon zest. Season with salt and pepper.
3. Break the egg into another shallow dish and beat together with the milk.
4. Dip the chicken pieces first into the egg and milk and then into the flour mixture, making sure they are well coated. Repeat so that the chicken has two coatings of flour. The chicken can be left to stand at this stage or cooked immediately.
5. Put the fat into a roasting tin and heat in the oven until sizzling. Arrange the chicken pieces, skin-side down, in the hot fat and cook for 20 minutes. Turn the pieces and cook for a further 20 minutes until crisp and golden brown. Drain on absorbent paper before serving.

SPICED CHICKEN WITH APRICOTS

30g/1oz dried apricots
oil for frying
2 chicken thighs
½ small onion, chopped
½ garlic clove, crushed
1 level teaspoon mild curry powder (see page 166)
150ml/¼ pint chicken stock (see page 162)
15g/½oz creamed coconut
1 tablespoon Greek yoghurt
salt and freshly ground black pepper
lemon or lime juice

To serve:
couscous (see page 73) or basmati rice (see page 70)

1. Soak the apricots in boiling water for 10 minutes. Heat the oil in a small frying pan and brown the chicken all over. Set aside.
2. Fry the onion in the oil until soft and transparent. Add the garlic and cook for 1 minute. Add the curry powder and stir over the heat for 1 further minute. Stir in the chicken stock and bring to the boil, stirring to remove any sediment from the bottom of the pan. Season with salt and pepper.
3. Drain the apricots, cut them in half, then place in the pan with the chicken. Cover and simmer gently for 30 minutes or until tender.
4. Chop up the creamed coconut and stir into the sauce with the yoghurt.

Add a squeeze of lemon or lime juice, season to taste and reheat without boiling. Serve with couscous or basmati rice.

NOTE: This recipe is also very good for using up the odd half of fresh mango or papaya instead of apricots.

❄ *Suitable for freezing at the end of stage 3. (Only freeze if using dried apricots.)*

MUSTARD AND PAPRIKA CHICKEN

2 chicken thighs
30g/1oz butter
1 tablespoon wholegrain mustard
squeeze of lemon juice
salt and freshly ground black pepper
½ teaspoon sugar
½ teaspoon paprika

1. Heat the grill to high. Wash the chicken and pat dry with absorbent paper.
2. Mix together the butter, mustard and lemon juice. Season with salt and pepper. Spread half the butter mixture over the underside of the chicken.
3. Grill for 10 minutes. Turn and spread the remaining butter on the skin side. Grill for a further 10 minutes. If the chicken is turning too dark before it is cooked, lower the grill pan. Check the chicken is cooked by piercing with a sharp knife: the juices should run clear.
4. Mix together the sugar and paprika. Sprinkle over the chicken and continue to grill until golden brown.

CHICKEN AND BACON PARCELS WITH GARLIC BEANS

2 boneless chicken thighs
salt and freshly ground black pepper
2 fresh sage leaves or sprigs of thyme
4 rashers streaky bacon, rind removed
1 garlic clove, chopped
55g/2oz green beans, top and tailed

1. Set the oven to 200°C/400°F/gas mark 6. Remove the skin from the chicken and rinse the meat under cold water. Trim any fat.
2. Season the chicken with salt and pepper. Place a sage leaf or sprig of thyme in the cavity left by the bone. Wrap two rashers of streaky bacon around each thigh. Place in a small roasting tin and bake for 30–40 minutes, until the bacon is brown and chicken cooked right through.
3. Transfer the chicken pieces to a warm plate. Set the roasting tin over the heat on top of the stove. Add the garlic and beans to the pan juices and fry gently for 2–3 minutes. Stir in a spoonful of water and allow to boil, scraping the sediment from the bottom of the pan. Cook until the liquid is reduced and just coats the beans. Check for seasoning and serve with the chicken.

ROSEMARY AND GARLIC CHICKEN WITH ROAST POTATOES

Buy a small whole bird and use the leftovers for chicken and broccoli crumble, gougère, or chicken tabouleh (see pages 95, 100 and 115).

SERVES 2
1 small chicken weighing about 1.25kg/
2lb 8oz
2 medium-sized potatoes, peeled
1 large garlic clove
salt and freshly ground black pepper
½ lemon
2 tablespoons olive oil
2 sprigs rosemary

1. Set the oven to 190°C/375°F/gas mark 5. Wash the chicken thoroughly and dry with absorbent paper.
2. Cut the potatoes in half, place in a pan of cold, salted water, bring to the boil and simmer for 2 minutes. Drain and leave to cool.
3. Crush the garlic with the back of a knife and rub all over the chicken. Place the chicken in a small roasting tin and season inside and out with salt and pepper.
4. Squeeze the juice from the lemon and spoon over the chicken with the olive oil. Cut the lemon rind into four and put into the cavity with the remains of the garlic and the rosemary.
5. Cook the chicken in the hot oven for 20 minutes, then add the potatoes, turning them in the hot oil. Continue to cook for a further hour, turning and basting the potatoes from time to time. The chicken is cooked when the juices run clear when the thigh is pierced.
5. Drain the juices from the pan and skim off the excess fat. Pour over the chicken and serve.

VARIATION
This recipe can also be made with a 340g/12oz poussin.

NOTE: If a lot of juice escapes from the chicken during the first 20 minutes of cooking roast the potatoes in a separate pan.

THAI GRILLED CHICKEN

2 chicken thighs

For the marinade:
30g/1oz creamed coconut
4 tablespoons boiling water
1 garlic clove, crushed
1 green chilli, deseeded and finely chopped (see page 15)
walnut-sized piece fresh ginger, peeled and finely chopped
zest and juice of ½ lime
1 tablespoon fresh chopped coriander
1 teaspoon finely chopped lemon grass

1. Make the marinade: slice the creamed coconut, dissolve in the boiling water and allow to become cold. Stir in the remaining marinade ingredients.
2. Wash the chicken thighs and remove the skin. Trim off any excess fat. Turn the chicken in the marinade, then cover and refrigerate for about 2 hours or overnight.
3. Heat the grill to its highest temperature. Place the chicken on the grill rack, spoon over some of the marinade and cook for 10–15 minutes, turning occasionally. The chicken is cooked when pierced and the juices run clear.

TURKEY BURGERS WITH GRILLED VEGETABLES

110g/4oz minced turkey
1 teaspoon olive oil
1 tablespoon rolled oats
1 heaped teaspoon chopped parsley
salt and freshly ground black pepper
lemon juice
pinch ground coriander
1 small courgette
½ red pepper, deseeded
onion wedge
olive oil for basting

To serve
ciabatta, focaccia or French bread
mayonnaise

1. Mix together the turkey, oil, oats and parsley. Season well with salt, pepper, a squeeze of lemon juice and a good pinch of coriander. Shape into a burger approximately 1cm/½ inch thick.
2. Heat the grill to its highest temperature. Wash the courgette and cut into lengthways strips. Cut the pepper into three and the onion in half. Brush all the vegetables with olive oil.
3. Grill the burger and the vegetables for 10–15 minutes until well browned.
4. A few minutes before they are done, cut the bread in half and warm it under the grill. Spread with mayonnaise, pop the burger inside and place the vegetables on top.

TURKEY STROGANOFF

170g/6oz turkey breast
15g/½oz unsalted butter
¼ onion, finely chopped
55g/2oz open mushrooms, sliced
1 tablespoon brandy or sherry
2 tablespoons chicken stock (see page 162)
salt and freshly ground black pepper
2 tablespoons crème fraîche
½ teaspoon Dijon or mild mustard

To serve:
pinch paprika

1. Trim the turkey breast and cut into 5cm/2 inch strips the width of a finger.
2. Melt the butter in a frying pan, add the turkey and fry briskly until browned on all sides. Add the onion and cook gently until soft and transparent, then add the mushrooms and continue to cook until softened.
3. If using brandy, pour it into the pan and set alight. Wait for the flames to die down. If using sherry, pour it into the pan and boil for 1 minute. Add the chicken stock, season with salt and pepper and stir over the heat for 2 minutes, until the turkey is cooked and the liquid well reduced.
1. Stir in the crème fraîche and mustard. Reheat, check for seasoning and serve sprinkled with a little paprika pepper.

AROMATIC TURKEY STIR-FRY

110g/4oz turkey breast
1–2 tablespoons sesame, stir-fry or sunflower oil
1 garlic clove, crushed
1 stem lemon grass, chopped
½ teaspoon coriander seeds, finely crushed
½ yellow pepper, deseeded and sliced
4 broccoli florets
5 baby corn, trimmed
1 carrot, peeled and cut into fine strips
4 radishes, roots removed, cut in half
1 tablespoon light soy sauce
1 tablespoon chicken or vegetable stock (see page 162–163)
salt and freshly ground black pepper

To serve:
basmati rice (see page 70) or noodles

1. Trim the turkey breast and cut it into strips about the size of a little finger.
2. Heat the oil in a wok or large frying pan. When hot, add the turkey strips and toss over the heat until browned on all sides. Add the garlic, lemon grass and coriander and fry for 1 minute.
3. Add all the vegetables and toss over the heat until hot but still crisp. Add the soy sauce and stock. Season with salt and pepper. Continue to stir over the heat until the liquid is reduced and syrupy. Serve immediately on a bed of rice or noodles.

GRILLED GUINEA FOWL WITH LIME BUTTER

SERVES 2
1 × 900g/2lb guinea fowl

For the marinade:
zest and juice of 1 lime
2 tablespoons oil
1 garlic clove, crushed
salt and freshly ground black pepper

To serve:
lime butter (see page 165)

1. Split the guinea fowl down one side of the backbone with a pair of poultry shears. Cut down the other side of the backbone to remove it completely. Now cut the guinea fowl in half through the breastbone. Place the two halves in a shallow dish.

2. Mix the marinade ingredients together and pour over the guinea fowl. Cover tightly and refrigerate overnight.

3. Heat the grill to its highest temperature and position the grill pan about 15cm/6 inches away from the heat. Lift the guinea fowl out of the marinade into a roasting tin. Grill for about 30 minutes in total, turning and basting three or four times with the marinade. The guinea fowl is cooked when the juices run clear from the thigh when pierced with a skewer. Serve immediately, topped with lime butter.

ROAST DUCK WITH ORANGE AND HONEY SALSA

The vibrant flavours of this dish are best offset by simple accompaniments such as a green salad or single green vegetable, lemon and thyme potatoes, or roast new potatoes with salt (see pages 147, 148 and 150).

1 × duckling leg joint
salt
1 orange
2 spring onions
½ red chilli, deseeded and finely chopped (see page 15)
squeeze of lime juice
1 teaspoon runny honey
1 tablespoon chopped fresh coriander

1. Set the oven to 200°C/400°F/gas mark 6. Prick the duckling joint all over and sprinkle lightly with salt. Set on a wire rack over a small roasting tin and roast for 30–40 minutes until tender.
2. Meanwhile, using a sharp knife, peel the orange as you would an apple, removing all the pith. Cut the flesh into segments, reserving all the juice and squeezing the pithy remains to remove the juice. Cut the segments into three and add to the juice. Trim the spring onions and cut into 2.5cm/1 inch lengths. Add to the orange with the chilli and lime juice. Stir in the honey and coriander.
3. When the duck is tender, remove it from the oven. Drain all the fat from the roasting tin and wipe out with absorbent paper. Put the duck back into the tin. Pour the orange and honey salsa over the duck and return to the oven for a further 10 minutes. Serve immediately.

DUCK STIR-FRY

1 boneless duck breast
55g/2oz green beans
½ red pepper, deseeded
1 teaspoon sugar
1 teaspoon cornflour
2 teaspoons light soy sauce
1 tablespoon sherry
1 tablespoon sesame oil
1cm/½ inch piece fresh ginger, peeled
and finely chopped
1 small red chilli, deseeded and finely
chopped (see page 15)
2 spring onions, trimmed and chopped
2 tablespoons chicken stock (see
page 162)
juice of ½ lime
salt and freshly ground black pepper

To serve:
basmati rice (see page 70) or noodles

1. Remove the skin and all the fat from the duck breast. Cut the flesh into finger-length strips. Top and tail the beans and cut into 2.5cm/1 inch pieces. Cut the red pepper into widthways strips. Mix together the sugar, cornflour, soy sauce and sherry.
2. Heat the oil in a wok. Add the duck, ginger and chilli and toss over a high heat for 2 minutes. Add the spring onions, beans and red pepper and fry for a further 2 minutes.
3. Add the cornflour mixture and stock and bring to the boil, stirring all the time. Season with salt, pepper and the lime juice. Serve with rice or noodles.

QUAIL BRAISED WITH RED CABBAGE AND PLUMS

Mashed potatoes with spring onions (see page 146) is the perfect accompaniment to this dish.

2 quail
salt and freshly ground black pepper
4 juniper berries
¼ red cabbage
½ red onion
110g/4oz fresh plums
1 tablespoon olive oil
30g/1oz sultanas
1 teaspoon brown sugar
1 teaspoon vinegar

1. Wash the quail. Season inside and out with salt and pepper. Crush the juniper berries and put one berry inside each quail.
2. Remove the stalk from the cabbage and slice the leaves finely. Immerse in cold water. Peel and finely slice the red onion. Stone and chop the plums roughly.
3. Heat the olive oil in a large, heavy-based pan and brown the quail all over. Set aside. Fry the onion gently until softened.
4. Drain the cabbage and place in the pan. Add the plums, sultanas, sugar, vinegar and remaining juniper berries. Season with salt and pepper and stir well.
5. Place the quail in the pan, embedding them well into the cabbage. Cover and simmer gently for 40 minutes, shaking and stirring from time to time. The cabbage should be dark and well cooked with all the liquid evaporated and the quail tender.

PORK, BEEF & LAMB

PORK, BEEF AND LAMB

This section offers a selection of recipes, some light on meat and some hearty ones too. As many people are now cautious about the amount of saturated fat they consume, the current trend is to serve smaller portions of red meat or to use meat sparingly to give flavour. The bulk of the meal comes from vegetables or pulses.

The recipes specify cuts of meat so that they may be easily ordered from a butcher or found ready-packed in supermarkets. If buying the latter it is a good idea to remove the wrapping, cover the meat loosely and store at the bottom of the refrigerator where it is cooler and the blood cannot drip on to any other food.

Animals raised for meat may be reared in various ways, and it is a matter of individual preference what type you buy. Meat from those reared outdoors or organically will, of course, cost rather more than intensively reared animals. Whichever you choose, look for pale pink pork, a plump cut of lamb with creamy white fat, or beef that is dull red with yellowish fat.

All recipes serve 1 unless stated otherwise.

PORK GOULASH WITH CARAWAY DUMPLINGS

225g/8oz boneless pork shoulder
oil for frying
½ medium-sized onion, finely sliced
1 teaspoon paprika
150ml/¼ pint chicken stock (see page 162)
225g/8oz tin tomatoes
salt and freshly ground black pepper
1 quantity caraway dumplings (see page 169)

To serve:
1 tablespoon soured cream or Greek yoghurt

1. Trim the pork and cut into 2.5cm/1 inch dice. Heat the oil in a heavy-based frying pan and brown the meat well on all sides. Transfer to a saucepan.
2. Add the onion to the pan and fry gently until golden brown. Stir in the paprika and cook for 1 minute. Place in the saucepan with the meat.
3. Pour the stock into the frying pan and

bring to the boil, stirring to remove any sediment from the bottom of the pan. Pour the liquid over the meat. Add the tomatoes, stir well and season with salt and pepper.

4. Bring to the boil and simmer gently for 40 minutes until the meat is tender.

5. About 20 minutes before the end of cooking, make the dumplings and drop into the simmering goulash. Cook gently for 10 minutes with the lid on and 10 minutes with the lid off. Serve straight away with a dollop of soured cream or Greek yoghurt.

❅ *Suitable for freezing at the end of stage 4.*

PORK POT ROAST

This traditional roast from a single pot makes a meal on its own, or it can be served with some freshly cooked green vegetables.

1 large carrot
1 medium-sized potato
1 parsnip
1 tablespoon dripping or oil
1 loin chop about 2.5cm/1 inch thick
salt and freshly ground black pepper
sprig fresh rosemary
1 level teaspoon flour
150ml/¼ pint chicken stock (see page 162)

1. Peel the vegetables. Cut the carrot into 2.5cm/1 inch pieces and the potato and parsnip into four.

2. Heat the dripping or oil in a heavy-based saucepan. Add the pork and fry until well browned all over. Scatter the vegetables around the pork, stirring well to give them a good coating of dripping. Season with salt and pepper and add the sprig of rosemary. Cover and cook, turning from time to time, over a very low heat for about 30 minutes, until the meat and vegetables are tender.

3. Transfer the meat and vegetables to a warm plate. Remove the sprig of rosemary. Sprinkle the flour into the pan juices and cook over the heat for 1 minute. Gradually add the stock, stirring until thick and boiling. Season with salt and pepper, pour over the meat and serve.

HAM AND MUSHROOM GOUGÈRE

This dish is a meal in itself, and the pastry is easy and quick to make.

SERVES 2
butter for greasing

For the choux pastry:
70g/2½oz plain flour
pinch dry mustard and cayenne pepper
salt and freshly ground black pepper
55g/2oz butter
150ml/¼ pint water
1 egg, beaten
1 tablespoon grated Parmesan cheese

For the filling:
15g/½oz butter
¼ onion, finely chopped
110g/4oz flat black mushrooms
15g/½oz plain flour
150ml/¼ pint chicken stock (see page 162)
2 tablespoons creamy milk
110–170g/4–6oz cooked ham, diced
grated Parmesan for sprinkling

To serve:
green salad (see page 150)

1. Set the oven to 200°C/400°F/gas mark 6. Grease a small ovenproof dish.
2. Make the pastry: sift the flour with the mustard and cayenne on to a sheet of absorbent paper. Season with salt and pepper. Put the butter and water in a pan and bring slowly to the boil. Immediately the liquid boils, slip all the flour mixture in at once, remove from the heat and beat until thick and coming away from the sides of the pan. Leave to cool, then beat in the egg and Parmesan. Alternatively, place the flour mixture in a food processor and process while pouring in the boiling water. Allow to cool, then beat in the egg and Parmesan. The mixture should be of a consistency that will drop reluctantly from a spoon.
3. Make the filling: melt the butter in a saucepan and fry the onion until soft and transparent. Add the mushrooms and fry until soft. Stir in the flour and cook for 1 minute. Gradually add the stock, stirring all the time until smooth and boiling. Add the milk and season with black pepper.
4. Spread the choux pastry around the sides of the greased dish. Pour the filling into the middle. Sprinkle the top with Parmesan. Bake for 40 minutes until the pastry is well risen and golden brown. Serve with a green salad.

VARIATION
This recipe is also good with the filling from chicken and broccoli crumble (see page 95).

❊ *The filling is suitable for freezing.*

PAN KEBABS

170g/6oz pork fillet or boneless loin
1 green pepper, deseeded

For the marinade:
1 tablespoon olive oil
2 tablespoons lemon juice
good pinch ground coriander and cumin
salt and freshly ground black pepper

To serve:
Greek yoghurt
tomato and cucumber wedges
red onion, sliced
basmati rice (see page 70) or pitta bread

1. Cut the pork and the pepper into 2.5cm/1 inch cubes. Mix all the marinade ingredients together. Pour over the pork and pepper. Cover and marinate overnight.

2. Drain the meat, reserving the marinade. Heat a heavy-based or non-stick frying pan until very hot. Add the pork and pepper and toss over the heat for about 10 minutes, until the meat is charred on the outside and cooked in the middle.

3. Transfer the meat and pepper to a warm plate. Pour the reserved marinade into the pan, stirring to remove the sediment, and boil until syrupy. Pour over the meat. Serve with a dollop of Greek yoghurt and the raw vegetables. This is good accompanied by rice or piled inside a piece of pitta bread along with the yoghurt and vegetables.

PORK AND CABBAGE COBBLER

SERVES 2
450g/1lb boneless pork shoulder
oil or dripping for frying
½ medium-sized onion, sliced
1 level teaspoon plain flour
290ml/½ pint chicken stock (see
page 162)
salt and freshly ground black pepper
1 small dessert apple, peeled, cored and
cut into cubes
110g/4oz white cabbage, finely
shredded
butter for greasing

For the cobbler:
110g/4oz self-raising flour
pinch dried mustard
55g/2oz suet

1. Trim the pork and cut into 2.5cm/1 inch cubes. Heat a little oil in a heavy-based frying pan and fry the pork briskly all over until well browned. Transfer to a saucepan.
2. Gently fry the onion until golden brown. Sprinkle in the flour and cook, stirring, for 1 minute. Spoon into the pan with the meat.
3. Put the chicken stock into the frying pan and bring to the boil, stirring to remove the sediment from the bottom of the pan. Pour over the meat, season with salt and pepper, bring to the boil and simmer gently for about 1 hour, or until the meat is tender. Stir in the apple and cabbage, then spoon the mixture into a greased pie dish.
4. Set the oven to 200°C/400°F/gas mark 6. Make the cobbler: sift the flour and mustard into a mixing bowl, then stir in the suet and season with salt and pepper. Mix with enough water to form a firm dough. On a floured worktop press the dough into a piece about 1cm/½ inch thick. Stamp out circles using a 5cm/2 inch cutter. Arrange the circles in an overlapping layer on top of the pork. Bake for 20–30 minutes, until the cobbler top has risen and browned.

❄ *Suitable for freezing at the end of stage 3.*

LOIN OF PORK WITH MOZZARELLA

The cheese in this recipe melts into a gooey sauce. Serve with crusty bread to mop up the juices and a green salad.

1 pork loin steak, approximately 170g/6oz
salt and freshly ground black pepper
1–2 teaspoons red pesto or sun-dried tomato paste
55g/2oz mozzarella, thinly sliced
2 teaspoons olive oil

1. Set the oven to 190°C/375°F/gas mark 5. Place the pork loin between two sheets of wet greaseproof paper and beat with a rolling pin until thin, like a veal escalope.
2. Season the flattened pork with salt and pepper, then spread with the red pesto. Arrange the sliced mozzarella on top.
3. Roll up the piece of pork and secure with a cocktail stick.
4. Heat the olive oil in a roasting tin and brown the pork roll all over. Bake in the oven for 30–40 minutes, until the meat is tender. Remove the cocktail stick and serve the pork immediately with any melted cheese from the bottom of the pan spooned over the top.

SAUSAGE HOT POT

SERVES 2
5 thick, good-quality meat sausages, about 340g/12oz in weight
340g/12oz butternut squash
2 teaspoons olive oil
½ medium onion, finely chopped
1 small leek, sliced
225g/8oz tin chopped tomatoes
150ml/¼ pint chicken stock (see page 162)
225g/8oz tin butter beans
salt and freshly ground black pepper
½ teaspoon dried marjoram or oregano
15g/½oz butter, melted

1. Set the oven to 200°C/400°F/gas mark 6. Twist the sausages in half. Peel and deseed the squash. Cut into 5mm/¼ inch slices.
2. Heat the oil in a heavy-based frying pan and brown the sausages all over. Drain on absorbent paper. Fry the onion and leek gently until golden brown.
3. Add the tomatoes and stock to the pan and bring to the boil, scraping any sediment from the bottom. Drain the butter beans and add to the pan with the browned sausages. Bring to the boil, season with salt, pepper and the herbs and pour into a small casserole dish.
4. Arrange the sliced squash in an overlapping layer on top of the sausage mixture and brush with melted butter. Cover and cook for 20 minutes, then uncover and cook for a further 20 minutes, until the top is golden brown.

GRILLED STEAK

Grill steak only if you have a powerful
and efficient grill, otherwise use the
pan-frying method. Choose a steak to
suit your appetite but one that is cut
about 2cm/¾ inch thick.

GRILLING TIMES FOR SIRLOIN AND RUMP
Blue: 1 minute per side
Rare: 1½ minutes per side
Medium rare: 2 minutes per side
Medium: 2½ minutes per side

GRILLING TIMES FOR FILLET STEAK
Blue: 1½ minutes per side
Rare: 2¼ minutes per side
Medium rare: 3¼ minutes per side
Medium: 4½ minutes per side

1 × rump, sirloin or fillet steak
oil
salt and freshly ground black pepper

To serve
quick hollandaise (see page 159), Stilton
butter (see page 165), mustard and mint
butter (see page 165) or a wedge of blue
Brie

1. Heat the grill to its highest
temperature and position the grill tray
on the highest rung. Brush the steak
with oil and season with pepper. Grill
the steak turning once and sprinkling
with salt.
2. Place the topping of your choice on
the steak and pop back under the grill
briefly to melt.

PAN-FRIED STEAK

1 × sirloin or fillet steak
salt and freshly ground black pepper
oil for frying
knob of butter

1. Season the steak with pepper. Brush a heavy-based frying pan with oil and heat until smoking. Brown the steak quickly on both sides. Sprinkle with salt, add the knob of butter and continue to cook for the required amount of time.

VARIATIONS

Serve the steak with a quick sauce made from pan juices.

Red wine sauce: Add 1 tablespoon full-bodied red wine and 1 tablespoon water to the hot pan. Allow to sizzle up and reduce to a syrupy sauce.

Mustard and basil sauce: Add 1 tablespoon water to the hot pan and stir, scraping the sediment from the bottom of the pan. Allow to sizzle up and reduce until syrupy. Stir in 1 tablespoon double cream or crème fraîche and 1 teaspoon wholegrain mustard. Bring to the boil, stir in six torn basil leaves and pour over the steak.

Peppercorn sauce: Add 1 tablespoon water to the hot pan, stirring to remove the sediment from the bottom of the pan. Bring to the boil and reduce. Add 1 teaspoon coarsely crushed, dried black or green peppercorns and 1 tablespoon double cream or crème fraîche. Mix well, bring to the boil and pour over the steak.

BURGERS

Home-made burgers make for a quick and simple supper. Use the best-quality mince or make your own by mincing lean steak in a food processor. (Don't over-process or the meat will become rubbery.) Although burgers can be made from 100 per cent beef, the addition of a little cereal helps retain moisture and flavour and makes for a juicier burger.

110–170g/4–6oz lean minced beef
1 teaspoon rolled oats
salt and freshly ground black pepper
ground nutmeg

To serve:
burger bun and side salad (see page 150)
or baked potato (see page 148) or lemon
and thyme baked potatoes (see page 148)
or tomato or avocado salsa (see
page 161)

Mix the beef with the oats. Season with salt, ground black pepper and nutmeg. Knead well and shape into a neat patty.

To fry: Brush a heavy-based frying pan with oil. Set over a high heat and when hot brown the burger on both sides. Turn the heat down and continue to cook for about 5 minutes a side for the meat to be cooked through but juicy.

To grill: Heat the grill to its highest temperature and grill the burger for about 5 minutes a side.

VARIATIONS

Spinach burger: Defrost 55g/2oz frozen leaf spinach, drain well and dry on absorbent paper. Chop roughly, then mix with 2 teaspoons fruit chutney and 1 teaspoon finely chopped onion. Knead into the basic burger mixture, then shape into a patty.

Chilli burger: To the basic burger recipe add 1 crushed garlic clove, 1 teaspoon chilli relish and ½ or whole fresh green or red chilli, deseeded and finely chopped (see page 15). Mix all the ingredients together and shape into a patty.

BOLOGNESE SAUCE

This recipe makes four servings, so freeze it in individual portions for future use.

1 tablespoon olive oil
450g/1lb minced beef
1 medium-sized onion, peeled and finely chopped
1 garlic clove, crushed
290–425ml/½–¾ pint chicken stock (see page 162)
900g/2lb tin tomatoes
2 teaspoons tomato purée
1 glass red wine (optional)
1 teaspoon dried basil or oregano
salt and freshly ground black pepper

1. Heat the oil in a heavy-based frying pan and fry the mince in batches until well browned all over. Transfer to a large saucepan.
2. Fry the onion gently until golden brown. Add the garlic and fry for a minute or two. Transfer both to the pan with the mince.
3. Pour the stock into the frying pan. Bring to the boil and stir, scraping any sediment from the bottom of the pan. Pour into the pan of meat. Add the tomatoes, tomato purée, wine (if using), herbs and seasoning.
4. Simmer for about 1 hour until well reduced to a rich sauce. Cool, then use or freeze as required.

TACOS

Taco shells are crisp corn tortillas folded in half to hold a filling. If the bolognese sauce is already made, this is a very quick but messy-to-eat supper! Serve with plenty of napkins and a hearty red wine.

4–5 taco shells
¼ quantity bolognese sauce (see page 122)
1 tablespoon chilli relish
sliced tomato
sliced cucumber
thin slices raw red onion
½ sliced avocado pear
55g/2oz Cheddar cheese, grated
handful shredded lettuce

1. Set the oven to 150°C/300°F/gas mark 2. Warm the taco shells for 5 minutes. Heat the bolognese sauce with the chilli relish until boiling and put into a dish. Arrange the sliced vegetables and grated cheese on a serving plate.
2. Put a spoonful or two of meat sauce into the bottom of the taco. Add some vegetables and top with cheese.

VEAL ESCALOPE WITH BALSAMIC VINEGAR

This would be equally good served with parsley pesto potatoes, tagliatelle or rice, and a green salad.

15g/½oz unsalted butter
1 × 140g/5oz veal escalope
1 tablespoon balsamic vinegar
1 tablespoon chicken stock (see page 162)
1 tablespoon crème fraîche
salt and freshly ground black pepper

1. Heat the butter in a heavy-based frying pan. When foaming, fry the veal escalope briskly for about 3 minutes a side. Transfer to a warm plate.
2. Pour the vinegar and stock into the pan. Allow to bubble up, stirring and scraping any sediment from the bottom of the pan. Add the crème fraîche and continue to stir to make a smooth sauce. Season with salt and pepper.
3. Return the veal escalope to the pan and turn in the sauce until reheated. Serve immediately.

GRILLED LAMB WITH MINTED AUBERGINES

1 neck fillet of lamb, approximately 170g/6oz
½ lemon
few sprigs thyme or marjoram
1 teaspoon coriander seeds, finely crushed
2 tablespoons olive oil
salt and freshly ground black pepper
1 small aubergine, sliced
1 tablespoon balsamic vinegar
1 teaspoon sugar
2 teaspoons chopped mint

1. Wash and trim the lamb fillet. Squeeze the juice from the lemon. Cut the lemon skin into four and add to the juice. Mix with the herbs, coriander seeds, oil, salt and pepper. Pour over the lamb, cover and leave to marinate for 3–4 hours or overnight.
2. Heat the grill to its highest temperature. Position the grill pan about 15cm/6 inches away from the heat. Cut the aubergine into 1cm/½ inch slices.
3. Arrange the lamb and sliced aubergine on the grill rack. Brush generously with the marinade. Grill for about 20 minutes, turning regularly to prevent burning and brushing with the marinade. Turn off the grill and leave to stand for 2 minutes.
4. Meanwhile, put the balsamic vinegar into a small pan and bring to the boil. Stir in the sugar and mint. Set aside.
5. Slice the lamb thickly. Pour the mint sauce over the aubergine and serve on the side.

LAMB STEAKS WITH REDCURRANTS

*1 leg of lamb steak, about 1cm/½ inch
thick
grated zest and juice of ½ orange
1 teaspoon olive oil
1 teaspoon balsamic vinegar
2 allspice, crushed
1 teaspoon chopped fresh coriander
salt and freshly ground black pepper
2 tablespoons chicken stock (see
page 162)
oil for frying
1 teaspoon redcurrant jelly
1 tablespoon fresh or frozen redcurrants
(optional)*

1. Trim the lamb steak. Mix together
the orange zest and juice, olive oil,
vinegar, allspice and coriander. Pour
over the lamb steaks, cover and leave to
marinate for several hours or overnight.
2. Drain the meat, reserving the
marinade, and season with salt and
pepper. Add the marinade to the
chicken stock.
3. Put a film of oil into a heavy-based
frying pan and heat until almost
smoking. Fry the lamb steak briskly on
both sides until dark brown. When
cooked, the meat should give a little
when pressed in the middle with the
fingertips. Transfer to a plate.
4. Pour the stock mixture into the frying
pan. Allow to sizzle up, stirring all the
time and scraping the sediment from the
bottom of the pan. Boil until reduced by
half. Add the redcurrant jelly and boil

until shiny and syrupy. Stir in the
redcurrants, if using, check for
seasoning and pour the sauce over the
lamb.

ITALIAN LAMB CASSEROLE

225g/8oz middle neck of lamb
1 carrot
1 small leek
1 tablespoon olive oil
½ medium-sized onion, peeled and sliced
1 garlic clove, crushed
290ml/½ pint chicken stock (see page 162)
15g/½oz dried green flageolet beans, soaked overnight
225/8oz tin tomatoes
salt and freshly ground black pepper
½ teaspoon dried oregano
½ courgette, diced

To serve:
parsley dumplings (see page 169) or parsley pesto potatoes (see page 146)

1. Trim the excess fat from the lamb. Peel the carrot and cut into 2.5cm/1 inch chunks. Trim the leek, wash thoroughly and cut into 2.5cm/1 inch pieces.
2. Heat the oil in a heavy-based frying pan and fry the lamb briskly on all sides until well browned. Transfer to a large saucepan.
3. Fry the onion gently until starting to brown. Stir in the garlic, carrot and leek and continue to cook until softened. Add to the pan of meat.
4. Pour the stock into the frying pan and bring to the boil, stirring and scraping any sediment from the bottom of the pan. Pour over the meat and vegetables.
5. Add the drained beans and the tomatoes. Season with salt, pepper and oregano. Bring to the boil and simmer gently for 1–1½ hours, stirring from time to time. The casserole is cooked when the meat falls easily from the bone.
6. Check for seasoning. Add the courgette. If serving with dumplings, add them now and cook for 10 minutes covered and 10 minutes uncovered. Alternatively, simmer for 10–15 minutes until the courgette pieces are tender.

❄ *Suitable for freezing at the end of stage 5.*

CHILLI LAMB STEAK

*1 leg of lamb steak, about 1cm/½ inch
thick*

For the marinade:
2 teaspoons hot water
½ teaspoon honey
6 mint leaves
*½ red chilli pepper, deseeded (see
page 15)*
walnut-sized piece fresh ginger, peeled
1 small garlic clove, peeled
1 teaspoon light soy sauce
freshly ground black pepper

1. Trim the lamb steak
2. Mix the hot water and honey
together and stir until dissolved. Chop
the mint, chilli, ginger and garlic and
add to the honey mixture. Stir in the soy
sauce and season with black pepper.
Pour over the lamb steak, cover and
refrigerate for several hours or
overnight.
3. Heat the grill to its highest
temperature. Grill the lamb steak for
about 4 minutes on each side, basting
with the marinade from time to time.
Serve with the grill pan juices poured
over.

LAMB WITH SPRING ONIONS AND HONEY

170g/6oz neck fillet of lamb
sesame or sunflower oil for frying
3 spring onions, sliced diagonally
*1 yellow or red pepper, deseeded and
sliced*
15g/½oz roasted peanuts
1 teaspoon grated fresh ginger
1 teaspoon light soy sauce
squeeze of lemon juice
1 teaspoon runny honey
salt and freshly ground black pepper

To serve:
basmati rice (see page 70) or noodles

For the garnish:
chopped fresh coriander

1. Wash and trim the lamb fillet and cut
into strips about the size of a little
finger. Heat some oil in a wok or heavy-
based frying pan. Add the lamb and fry
briskly for 3–4 minutes until browned
all over and cooked through. Transfer
to a warm plate.
2. Add the spring onions, pepper,
peanuts and ginger to the juices in the
pan. Toss over the heat for 1 minute.
Stir in the soy sauce, lemon juice and
honey. Bring to the boil, season to taste
and pour over the meat. Garnish with
fresh coriander and serve immediately
with noodles or rice.

RACK OF LAMB WITH LETTUCE AND BEANS

1 × 3 cutlet rack of lamb, chined,
trimmed and skinned
1 teaspoon wholegrain mustard
1 teaspoon brown sugar
salt and freshly ground black pepper
handful washed and shredded crisp
lettuce
1 × 225g/8oz tin butter beans
1 teaspoon fresh chopped mint

1. Set the oven to 220°C/425°F/gas
mark 7. Trim the excess fat from the
lamb. Using a sharp knife, score the
remaining fat with criss-cross slashes.
Spread the mustard over the skin, then
press on the brown sugar. Season with
salt and pepper. Roast for 10–15
minutes for slightly pink meat.
2. Dry the lettuce well with absorbent
paper. Drain the butter beans. Lift the
lamb on to a warm plate. Pour off the
excess fat from the roasting tin and set
the pan over the heat on top of the
stove. Add the lettuce and beans. Season
with salt and pepper. Toss over the heat
in the pan juices, until the lettuce is
wilted and the beans are hot. Stir in the
chopped mint and spoon on to the plate
beside the lamb.

LAMB FILLETS WITH YOGHURT AND TOMATO

170g/6oz lamb neck fillet
oil for frying
1 garlic clove, chopped
3 tablespoons chicken stock (see
page 162)
2 fresh tomatoes, peeled and quartered
1 tablespoon chopped fresh coriander
salt and freshly ground black pepper
pinch sugar
2 tablespoons Greek yoghurt

To serve:
basmati rice (see page 70)

1. Trim and slice the lamb fillets about
1cm/½ inch thick. Heat the oil in a
heavy-based frying pan and briskly
brown the lamb on all sides. Add the
garlic and fry for 1 minute. Transfer to
a saucepan. Pour the stock into the
frying pan and bring to the boil, stirring
to remove the sediment from the
bottom of the pan. Pour over the meat.
2. Scatter the tomatoes and coriander
over the meat and season with salt,
pepper and sugar. Cover and simmer
for 30–40 minutes, until the meat is
tender.
3. Stir in the yoghurt and check for
seasoning. Serve with rice.

❄ *Suitable for freezing at the end of*
stage 2.

PAN-FRIED LAMB WITH MUSHROOMS AND GARLIC

3 lamb cutlets
olive oil for frying
1 garlic clove, chopped
110g/4oz horse, chestnut or flat black
mushrooms, thickly sliced
salt and freshly ground black pepper
1 teaspoon fresh chopped rosemary
1 tablespoon sherry
1 tablespoon water

1. Trim any excess fat from the lamb. Brush a heavy-based frying pan with oil and set over a high heat. When hot, brown the lamb well on both sides.
2. Turn down the heat and fry the garlic and mushrooms. Season with salt and pepper and sprinkle in the rosemary. Fry gently, stirring from time to time and turning the lamb, until the mushrooms are cooked and the meat is done to your liking. Spoon on to a warm plate.
3. Turn the heat up high and add the sherry and water. Allow to bubble, stirring to remove any sediment from the bottom of the pan. Boil to a spoonful of reduced, syrupy sauce. Pour over the lamb and serve.

CALVES' LIVER SMOTHERED WITH ONIONS

This is delicious with mashed potato or pasta.

85g/3oz calves' liver, very thinly sliced
30g/1oz butter
½ medium onion, thinly sliced
4 sage leaves or 1 teaspoon fresh thyme
salt and freshly ground black pepper
1 tablespoon red wine or sherry
1 tablespoon chicken stock (see
page 162)

1. Remove any skin or membrane from the liver.
2. Heat half the butter in a heavy-based frying pan and fry the onion slowly until deep golden brown. This will take at least 10 minutes. Spoon on to a plate and keep warm.
3. Melt the remaining butter in the same pan and briskly fry the liver for about 1 minute on each side. Scatter the sage or thyme on top and season with salt and pepper while frying. Place the liver on top of the onions.
4. Add the wine and stock to the hot pan and boil until reduced and syrupy. Pour over the liver and serve straight away.

SPICED LIVER STIR-FRY

110g/4oz chicken livers
1 tablespoon balsamic vinegar
1 teaspoon oil
½ teaspoon ground cumin
½ green chilli, deseeded and finely chopped (see page 15)
salt and freshly ground black pepper
30g/1oz green beans, topped and tailed
2 rashers streaky bacon
1 tablespoon chicken stock (see page 162)

To serve:
basmati rice (see page 70) or couscous (see page 73)

1. Rinse the livers and trim away any discoloured pieces. Mix together the vinegar, oil, cumin and chilli. Add the livers, season with a little salt, cover and marinate for 30 minutes to 2 hours.
2. Cut the beans into 2.5cm/1 inch pieces. Discard the rind from the bacon and cut into 1cm/½ inch pieces. Drain the livers, reserving the marinade.
3. Heat a wok or heavy-based frying pan. When hot, add the bacon and fry until browned. Add the livers and fry briskly for about 2 minutes, until dark brown and caramelized on the outside but still pink in the middle.
4. Add the beans. Pour in the marinade and chicken stock and allow to bubble up. Season with salt and pepper. Stir well until the liquid is reduced and syrupy. Serve immediately with rice or couscous.

KIDNEYS WITH APPLE AND MUSTARD

2 lambs' kidneys
15g/½oz butter
½ small onion, chopped
1 small dessert apple
squeeze of lemon juice
1 tablespoon sherry
1 tablespoon crème fraîche
1 teaspoon wholegrain mustard
salt and freshly ground black pepper
2 teaspoons chopped parsley

To serve:
mashed potatoes with spring onions (see page 146) or basmati rice (see page 70)

1. Skin the kidneys, halve them and snip out the core with a pair of scissors. Cut into thin slices.
2. Heat the butter in a heavy-based frying pan. Add the onion and cook gently until lightly browned. Meanwhile, peel and core the apple and slice thickly. Add to the pan with the onion. Season with lemon juice and set aside.
3. In the same pan fry the kidneys briskly for a few minutes until well browned. Add the sherry and bring to the boil, scraping any sediment from the bottom of the pan.
4. Return the onion and apple to the pan. Add the crème fraîche and mustard and mix well. Bring to the boil and simmer gently for 4–5 minutes. Season with salt and pepper. Sprinkle liberally with chopped parsley. Serve with mashed potatoes or rice.

VEGETARIAN MAIN
COURSES

VEGETARIAN MAIN COURSES

This section is not aiming to provide authoritative vegetarian cooking, but simply a small selection of dishes that do not include meat or fish. Most of the following recipes make a meal on their own if served with crusty bread. Rice, couscous, baked potatoes or salad would also be suitable accompaniments. Meat-eaters might like to try some recipes as a side dish, in which case there would be enough for two people.
All recipes serve 1 unless stated otherwise.

SPICED BLACK-EYED BEANS AND POTATOES

SERVES 2
110g/4oz black-eyed beans, soaked overnight
1 tablespoon sunflower oil
1 medium-sized onion, sliced
walnut-sized piece fresh ginger, peeled and chopped finely
1 garlic clove, crushed
1 teaspoon garam marsala (see page 167)
½ teaspoon each ground turmeric, coriander and cumin
2 fresh green chillies, deseeded and chopped (see page 15)
425ml/¾ pint vegetable stock (see page 163)
salt and freshly ground black pepper
1 large waxy potato
large handful fresh coriander, roughly chopped
1 tomato, peeled and chopped

1. Drain the beans. Heat the oil in a heavy-based pan, add the onion and fry gently until soft and golden brown. Add the ginger and garlic and fry for a further minute. Add the spices and fresh chilli and stir over the heat for another minute.
2. Pour in the vegetable stock and season with pepper. Bring to the boil, add the beans and simmer for 1 hour.
3. Peel the potato and cut into 1cm/½ inch dice. Add to the beans and season with salt. Cook for about 15 minutes, until the potatoes are tender.
4. Stir in the coriander and tomato and reheat before serving.

LENTIL SHEPHERD'S PIE

SERVES 2

55g/2oz green lentils
1 leek
1 carrot, peeled
1 tomato, peeled
1 tablespoon sunflower oil
1 small onion, peeled and diced
dash tomato purée
290ml/½ pint vegetable stock (see page 163)
salt and freshly ground black pepper
pinch sugar
2 quantities mashed potato with spring onion (see page 146)
1 tablespoon grated Cheddar cheese

1. Soak the lentils for 2–3 hours. Remove the outer skin from the leek and wash thoroughly. Cut the leek and carrot into 1cm/½ inch chunks. Chop the tomato.
2. Heat the oil in a saucepan. Gently fry the onion until soft and lightly browned. Add the leek and carrot and continue to fry for 5 minutes. Stir in the soaked lentils, tomato purée and stock. Season with salt, pepper and sugar. Bring to the boil, then simmer gently for 40 minutes, until the vegetables are tender and the liquid is reduced and syrupy.
3. Set the oven to 200°C/400°F/gas mark 6. Spoon the lentil mixture into an ovenproof dish. Spread the mashed potato on top. Sprinkle with grated cheese. Cook in the hot oven for about 20 minutes, until crisp and golden brown.

❄ *Suitable for freezing.*

WARM MUSHROOM AND POTATO SALAD

1 little gem lettuce
1 tablespoon chopped chives
handful of rocket, if available
110g/4oz flat, chestnut or shiitake
mushrooms
85g/3oz cooked new potatoes
2 tablespoons olive oil
110g/4oz broccoli florets
salt and freshly ground black pepper
2 teaspoons balsamic vinegar

To serve:
fresh bread

1. Discard the outer lettuce leaves, then cut into quarters, wash and pat dry with absorbent paper. Put the lettuce into a bowl with the chives and rocket.
2. Thickly slice the mushrooms and potatoes. Heat the oil in a heavy-based pan and briskly fry the potatoes until browned. Use a draining spoon to transfer them to the salad bowl. Briskly fry the mushrooms.
3. Meanwhile, lightly boil the broccoli and drain it. Add to the bowl of lettuce.
4. Add the mushrooms, including the hot oil, to the lettuce mixture. Season with salt and pepper and toss with the balsamic vinegar. Serve immediately with fresh bread.

ROAST VEGETABLES WITH PINENUTS

This recipe makes a complete meal for one if served with crusty bread, or serves two if accompanied by a main course.

1 small onion
1 courgette
1 small red pepper
1 medium-sized potato
good pinch dried oregano or marjoram
salt and freshly ground black pepper
3 tablespoons olive oil
1 tomato, cut in half
1 tablespoon pinenuts

To serve:
fresh, crusty bread

1. Preheat the oven to 190°C/375°F/gas mark 5. Peel and halve the onion. Trim the stalk and root.
2. Wash the other vegetables. Trim the courgette and cut in half lengthways. Cut the pepper in half, leaving the stalk on, and remove the seeds and membranes. Cut the potato in half lengthways.
3. Put all the vegetables into a roasting tin. Sprinkle with the herbs, salt and pepper. Spoon over the olive oil and turn the vegetables until evenly coated.
4. Bake in the hot oven for 40 minutes, turning from time to time. Add the tomato and sprinkle the pinenuts over the whole dish. Return to the oven for another 20 minutes. The vegetables should be well cooked and charred at the edges.

MEXICAN BEAN POT

SERVES 2
110g/4oz pinto beans, soaked overnight
1 tablespoon sunflower oil
1 medium onion, peeled and sliced
1 level teaspoon ground cumin
1 or 2 green chillies, deseeded and finely sliced (see page 15)
1 green pepper, deseeded and sliced
1 red pepper, deseeded and sliced
150ml/¼ pint black coffee
400g/14oz tin tomatoes
1 teaspoon black treacle
1 teaspoon dried oregano
salt and freshly ground black pepper

1. Drain the beans and place in a large saucepan. Heat the oil in a heavy-based frying pan. Add the onions and fry gently until golden brown. Stir in the cumin and cook for a further minute.
2. Add the chillies and peppers, stir, then cover and fry gently for about 10 minutes until soft.
3. Add the coffee, tomatoes, treacle and oregano and season with black pepper. Stir well, bring to the boil and pour into the pan with the beans. Simmer for 1–1½ hours. Season with salt. The beans should be soft and tender and the liquid well reduced and syrupy.

❄ *Suitable for freezing.*

RATATOUILLE WITH CHICK PEAS

SERVES 2
55g/2oz chick peas, soaked overnight
1 small aubergine
1 courgette
1 red pepper
1 green pepper
1 tablespoon olive oil
1 medium-sized onion, sliced
1 garlic clove, peeled and crushed
400g/14oz tin tomatoes
1 teaspoon dried basil
salt and freshly ground black pepper

1. Drain the chick peas. Put into a pan with fresh water and boil for 10 minutes.
2. Wipe the aubergine and courgette. Deseed the peppers. Cut them all into 2.5cm/1 inch chunks.
3. Heat the oil in a saucepan and gently fry the onion until soft. Add the garlic and fry for 1 minute. Stir in the courgette, aubergine and peppers, then cover and sweat for about 15 minutes.
4. Drain the chick peas and add to the vegetables with the tomatoes and basil. Season with salt and pepper. Simmer gently for about 45 minutes, until the chick peas are tender.

❄ *Suitable for freezing.*

VARIATION
Serve topped with a poached egg and grated cheese.

GRILLED AUBERGINES

1 large aubergine, washed and dried
1 garlic clove, peeled and crushed
1 tablespoon capers, well rinsed and
chopped
1 tablespoon chopped fresh coriander
1 shallot or spring onion, finely
chopped
grated zest and juice of ½ lemon
2 tablespoons olive oil
salt and freshly ground black pepper

To serve:
crusty bread
side salad (see page 150) or Greek salad
(see page 149)

1. Cut the aubergine into 1cm/½ inch
slices.
2. Put the garlic, capers, coriander,
shallot, lemon zest and juice in a bowl.
Warm the oil in a saucepan and pour
into the bowl.
3. Heat the grill to its highest
temperature. Brush the aubergine slices
with some of the dressing. Grill until
deep golden brown on both sides,
brushing with more dressing when
turned.
4. Put the aubergine on a plate and pour
over the remaining dressing. Serve with
plenty of crusty bread and a salad.

ROAST RED PEPPERS WITH GOATS' CHEESE

Serves 1 as a main course or 2 as a side
dish.

1 large red pepper
1 large tomato, peeled
1 garlic clove, peeled
good pinch oregano or marjoram
salt and freshly ground black pepper
1 tablespoon olive oil
55g/2oz goats' cheese

1. Preheat the oven to 190°C/375°F/gas
mark 5. Wash the pepper, cut in half
with the stalk on and remove the
membrane and seeds. Cut the tomato
into quarters and the garlic into slivers.
2. Put the pepper, cut side up, into a
small roasting tin. Put two quarters of
tomato into each pepper. Scatter with
the garlic and herbs, and season with
salt and pepper. Spoon half the olive oil
into each pepper. Bake in the oven for
30 minutes.
3. Break the goats' cheese in half and
crumble into the peppers. Baste with the
cooking juices and return to the oven
for a further 15–20 minutes until
beginning to brown on top.

MILD VEGETABLE CURRY

This is a creamy curry. If a hotter dish is preferred, add extra cayenne pepper and fresh chilli.

1 tablespoon sunflower oil
½ medium onion, finely chopped
pinch cumin seed
pinch black mustard seed
½ level teaspoon turmeric
pinch cayenne pepper
1 garlic clove, crushed
½ green pepper, deseeded and sliced
1 small carrot, peeled and cut into sticks
1 small courgette, cut into sticks
4 small cauliflower florets
1 green chilli, deseeded and chopped finely (see page 15)
30g/1oz coconut cream
290ml/½ pint boiling water or vegetable stock (see page 163)
salt and freshly ground black pepper
1 tablespoon chopped fresh coriander

To serve:
couscous (see page 73), basmati rice (see page 70) or hot naan bread

1. Heat the oil in a pan. Add the cumin and mustard seed and fry until beginning to pop. Add the onion and sweat until beginning to soften. Turn up the heat and fry until golden brown. Stir in the turmeric and cayenne and fry for 1 minute. Add the garlic and cook for 1 further minute.

2. Stir in the pepper, carrot, courgette, cauliflower and chilli until well coated with the spice and onion mixture.

3. Dissolve the creamed coconut in the boiling water or stock. Pour over the vegetables. Season with salt and pepper, cover and simmer gently until the vegetables are tender and the liquid has reduced to a creamy sauce. This should take about 20 minutes. Sprinkle with fresh coriander before serving with rice, couscous or naan bread.

COURGETTE TOAD IN THE HOLE WITH TOMATO CHILLI PURÉE

SERVES 2

1 large courgette or butternut squash, or
a mixture of the two
1 tablespoon sunflower oil
½ medium onion, sliced

For the batter:
55g/2oz plain flour
pinch salt
good pinch dried tarragon
1 egg
150ml/¼ pint milk and water, mixed
half and half

For the purée:
1 large tomato
1 fresh green chilli (see page 15)
15g/½oz butter
salt and freshly ground black pepper
pinch sugar

1. Set the oven to 220°C/425°F/gas mark 7. Make the batter by sifting the flour into a mixing bowl. Add the salt and tarragon. Make a well in the centre and break the egg into this. Add a little of the milk and mix with a wooden spoon or whisk, gradually drawing in the flour from the sides. When the mixture reaches the consistency of thick cream, beat well and stir in the rest of the milk. (The batter can also be made by whizzing all the ingredients together in a liquidizer or food processor.) Set aside.

2. Cut the courgette diagonally into 1cm/½ inch slices, or peel the squash and cut into four lengthways pieces. Remove the seeds and cut the flesh into thick slices. Place a small roasting tin on top of the stove and heat the oil. Add the onion and cook gently until softened. Turn up the heat, add the courgette or squash and toss over the heat for 1 minute. Pour in the batter and put into the hot oven for 20–30 minutes. The 'toad' is cooked when the batter is well risen and golden brown.

3. Meanwhile, peel and chop the tomato. Deseed and chop the chilli. When the toad is nearly cooked, melt the butter in a small, heavy-based pan. Add the tomato and chilli and toss over the heat until any liquid has boiled away and the tomato has reduced to a thickish purée. Season with salt and pepper and a pinch of sugar.

4. Serve the toad straight away with the tomato chilli purée on the side.

NEW POTATO AND FETA CHEESE SALAD

225g/8oz new potatoes
salt and freshly ground black pepper
sprig of mint
2 tablespoons olive oil
1 teaspoon balsamic vinegar
6 cherry tomatoes, halved
6 black or green olives, stoned
30g/1oz feta cheese, crumbled
2 spring onions, cleaned and chopped
pinch oregano

To serve:
green salad (see page 150)

1. Scrub the new potatoes and cook in boiling salted water with the sprig of mint for about 10 minutes. The potatoes should be cooked but still firm.
2. While still hot, cut the potatoes in half and toss in the olive oil and vinegar. Add the cherry tomatoes, olives, cheese and spring onions. Season with oregano and plenty of black pepper. Use only a little salt as the cheese may be salty. Mix gently.

VARIATION
This salad can also be served hot. Set the oven to 220°C/425°F/gas mark 7. Spoon the salad into a shallow, ovenproof dish and bake for about 15 minutes, until the potatoes are slightly browned. Serve inside warm pitta bread.

CHEATS' CHEESE SOUFFLÉ

Making a traditional soufflé for just one person is a little fiddly, but this recipe makes it easy, although the result is more like a light, cheesy bread pudding puffed up with lots of egg white. It makes a delicious supper with a selection of fresh vegetables.

15g/½oz butter plus extra for greasing
generous 30g/1oz fresh white
breadcrumbs
1 large egg
6 tablespoons milk
45g/1½oz Cheddar cheese, finely grated
¼ teaspoon English mustard
salt and freshly ground black pepper

1. Heat the oven to 180°C/350°F/gas mark 4. Grease a 290ml/½ pint soufflé dish with some butter, then sprinkle with 1 teaspoon breadcrumbs so that the inside of the dish is coated.
2. Separate the egg into 2 bowls. Lightly beat the yolk with a fork.
3. Put the milk and butter into a small pan and warm slightly. Pour on to the egg yolk, stirring all the time, then stir in the rest of the breadcrumbs, the cheese and the mustard. Season to taste and leave for 5 minutes to allow the breadcrumbs to swell.
4. Whisk the egg white until it forms soft peaks. Fold into the cheese mixture, pour into the prepared dish and bake in the oven for 30–35 minutes until risen and golden. Serve immediately

(although it won't sink anywhere near as quickly as a conventional soufflé).

VARIATIONS
Spinach soufflé: Stir in 110g/4oz well-drained and roughly chopped spinach before adding the egg whites.
Mediterranean soufflé: Use 30g/1oz finely grated Parmesan or pecorino cheese instead of the Cheddar and ½ teaspoon pesto sauce instead of the mustard. Stir in together with 2 sliced spring onions, 15g/½oz sliced sun-dried tomatoes preserved in oil and 1 tablespoon toasted pinenuts before adding the egg whites.
Stilton soufflé: Use finely grated Stilton instead of Cheddar and stir in with 1 teaspoon finely chopped parsley before adding the egg whites.

VEGETABLES, SALADS, SNACKS & SIDE DISHES

VEGETABLES, SALADS, SNACKS AND SIDE DISHES

In Britain vegetables are usually served as an accompaniment to a main dish. There is, however, no need for all meals to be the traditional combination of meat, potatoes and two veg. Meat or fish with lots of vegetables are great, and so is a plateful of assorted vegetables simply topped with a savoury butter.

Always wash vegetables before preparing them, but do not cut them up or leave soaking in water for ages before use. This will simply allow the vitamins and minerals they contain to leach out.

Do remember that most vegetables require little cooking. Boil them, separately, in water that has come to a rolling boil and which barely covers them. Leafy green vegetables, such as cabbage, kale or spinach, should be cooked in about 4mm/⅛ inch boiling water in a tightly covered pan so that they cook in steam. The residual water contains plenty of flavour and nutrients, so reserve it for a sauce or gravy.

Steaming is a good method of cooking vegetables, especially small quantities of root vegetables, because it retains maximum flavour and nutrients. A medley of vegetables can be steamed in one pot, added in sequence, according to how long they take to cook. Flexible stainless steel steaming baskets can be bought that will fit into most sizes of saucepan.

Microwave ovens are also handy for cooking vegetables. Beans, carrots, courgettes, mangetout, fresh peas and sweetcorn are all particularly successful. If you fancy something other than plainly cooked vegetables, see the following recipes.

All recipes serve 1 unless stated otherwise.

MASHED POTATO WITH SPRING ONIONS

285g/10oz floury potatoes
2 spring onions, cleaned
1 tablespoon soured cream or Greek
yoghurt
15g/½ oz butter
salt and freshly ground black pepper
ground nutmeg

1. Peel the potatoes and cut into even-sized pieces. Boil gently in salted water until tender. Drain thoroughly. Chop the onions finely.
2. Return the potatoes to the dry saucepan and set over a low heat. Mash with a large fork or potato masher, allowing the potato steam to evaporate.
3. Sir in the soured cream or yoghurt and butter. Add the spring onions and season to taste with salt, pepper and nutmeg.

PARSLEY PESTO POTATOES

4–6 new potatoes
salt and freshly ground black pepper
1 tablespoon olive oil
1 garlic clove, peeled and chopped
1 teaspoon pinenuts
1 heaped teaspoon chopped fresh
parsley
pinch grated Parmesan cheese

1. Wash the new potatoes and, if necessary, cut into even-sized pieces. Boil in salted water until tender.
2. When the potatoes are cooked, drain them and set aside. Heat the olive oil in the pan and gently fry the garlic and pinenuts until beginning to take on colour. Return the potatoes to the pan and mix well. Toss in the parsley and Parmesan and season with salt and pepper.

ROAST NEW POTATOES WITH SALT

225g/8oz even-sized new potatoes
2 tablespoons olive oil
2 teaspoons rock salt

1. Set the oven to 200°C/400°F/gas mark 6. Scrub the potatoes and pat dry. Put into a baking tin with the oil and turn until they are evenly coated. Sprinkle with the rock salt.
2. Bake for about 40 minutes, until the potatoes are tender and the skins crisp and brown. Drain on absorbent paper before serving.

QUICK DAUPHINOISE POTATOES

SERVES 2
butter for greasing
285g/10oz waxy potato
150ml/¼ pint double cream
2 tablespoons milk
1 small garlic clove, crushed
salt and freshly ground black pepper
freshly grated nutmeg
1 tablespoon grated Parmesan cheese

1. Set the oven to 190°C/375°F/gas mark 5. Grease a small ovenproof dish with butter.
2. Peel and finely slice the potatoes. Mix the cream, milk and garlic together and season with salt, pepper and nutmeg.
3. Put the sliced potatoes into the bowl with the cream and milk mixture and stir well. Pile into the prepared dish and sprinkle with the Parmesan cheese. Bake for 45 minutes until the potatoes are cooked through and golden brown on top.

LEMON AND THYME BAKED POTATOES

1 large, waxy potato weighing about 285g/10oz
salt and freshly ground black pepper
2 tablespoons olive oil
grated zest of 1 lemon
1 teaspoon fresh thyme or good pinch dried thyme

1. Cut the unpeeled potato into four. Parboil in salted water for about 10 minutes. The potato should still be quite firm. Cool.
2. Preheat the oven to 220°C/425°F/gas mark 7. Brush a shallow, ovenproof dish with a little olive oil. Cut the potato into 0.5cm/¼ inch slices, leaving the skin on. Arrange in an overlapping layer in the oiled dish.
3. Sprinkle the lemon zest and thyme over the potato and season with salt and pepper. Brush liberally with all the remaining oil.
4. Bake in the hot oven for about 30 minutes until cooked all the way through and golden brown on top.

BAKED POTATOES

To bake a potato in a conventional oven: set the oven to 200°C/400°F/gas mark 6. Prick a washed potato with a fork and bake for 1 hour or until a skewer glides through easily.
To bake a potato in a microwave oven: prick a washed potato with a fork. Wrap in absorbent paper and microwave on High for 6 minutes. Allow to stand for 3 minutes.
To bake a potato in a combination oven: prick a washed potato with a fork and cook on 200°C/High power microwave for 6 minutes. Allow to stand for 3 minutes.

SERVING SUGGESTIONS

- Cottage cheese and chopped spring onions
- Ratatouille with chick peas (see page 136)
- Scrambled egg and smoked ham or smoked salmon (see page 54)
- Spinach, pinenuts and raisins (see page 63)
- Sicilian sauce (see page 65)
- ¼ quantity bolognese sauce (see page 122)
- 110g/4oz frozen spinach defrosted and cooked in 15g/½oz butter until all the moisture has evaporated. Stir in 1 teaspoon grated Parmesan cheese and top with a poached egg.
- 1 × 110g/4oz tin tuna, drained and flaked. Mix with 2 teaspoons fromage frais or mayonnaise, chopped red onion and 1 tablespoon tinned butter beans.

GREEK SALAD

This salad can be served as a snack or lunch dish with good fresh bread, or as an accompaniment to a main course, particularly grilled or pan-fried meat dishes.

1 little gem lettuce
¼ cucumber
1 ripe tomato
55g/2oz feta cheese
¼ small red onion, peeled and thinly sliced
1 tablespoon kalamata olives
salt and freshly ground black pepper
few leaves flat parsley or fresh coriander
extra virgin olive oil
lemon juice

1. Discard the outer lettuce leaves and cut the remainder into four. Wash well and dry. Arrange on a serving plate.
2. Cut the cucumber in half lengthways and then into thick slices. Cut the tomato into eighths and the feta cheese into 1cm/½ inch dice.
3. Scatter the cucumber, tomato, cheese, onion and olives over the lettuce. Grind salt and black pepper over the salad, dot with the parsley or coriander and drizzle with olive oil and lemon juice.

TOMATO, AVOCADO AND MOZZARELLA SALAD

Serves 1 as main course or 2 as a side salad
1 small, ripe avocado pear
85g/3oz mozzarella, sliced
1 tomato, peeled and sliced
salt and freshly ground black pepper
1 teaspoon balsamic vinegar
2 teaspoons olive oil
1 teaspoon torn basil leaves

1. Peel and slice the avocado. Arrange in overlapping slices on a plate. Arrange the sliced mozzarella and then the tomato next to the avocado.
2. Season with salt and pepper. Drizzle balsamic vinegar and olive oil over the top and scatter with basil leaves.

SIDE SALADS

There is a great choice of salad leaves available from supermarkets, including lettuce, watercress, curly endive, young spinach, chicory, lambs' lettuce and rocket. Any one or combination will be suitable as the basis of a salad. Little gem lettuce are ideally suited for use in small quantities. Most lettuce varieties store well if refrigerated, but do not prepare them until needed or the leaves will wilt and brown at the edges. Pre-washed and packed salad assortments are ideal for one or two people.

Additional salad ingredients: sliced cucumber, sliced fennel, chopped celery, spring onions, fresh herbs, tomatoes, carrot ribbons (keep peeling with a potato peeler), raw mushrooms or avocado pear.

For a more filling salad add: shavings of Parmesan, hardboiled quails' eggs (boil for 3 minutes), softboiled eggs (boil for 5 minutes), tinned kidney beans or crisp bacon.

TOMATO SALAD

2 ripe but firm tomatoes, or 8 cherry tomatoes, or a mix of the two
1 teaspoon finely chopped red onion
squeeze of orange juice or sprinkle of balsamic vinegar
1 teaspoon olive oil
salt and freshly ground black pepper

1. Finely slice the tomatoes or half the cherry tomatoes. Add the onion, orange juice and oil, season with salt and pepper and mix well.

Ham and Mushroom Gougère

Italian Lamb Casserole with Parsley Dumplings

Roast Rack of Lamb with Lettuce and Beans

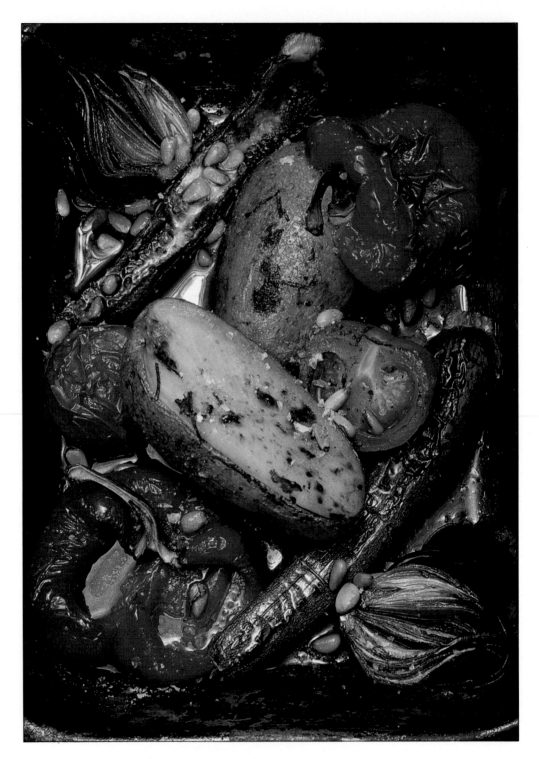

Roast Vegetables with Pinenuts

Baked Blue Cheese Mushrooms

Pears Savoyard

Marmalade Pudding

Grilled Berry Meringue

LENTILS WITH GARLIC AND TOMATO

SERVES 2
1 tablespoon olive oil
1 teaspoon cumin seeds
1 large onion, finely chopped
1 garlic clove, crushed
25g/8oz tin chopped tomatoes
55g/2oz green lentils
290ml/½ pint chicken or vegetable stock
(see page 162–163)
salt and freshly ground black pepper

1. Heat the olive oil in a heavy-based frying pan. Add the cumin seeds and fry until they begin to pop. Add the chopped onion and fry gently until soft and transparent. Stir in the garlic and cook for a further minute.
2. Add the tomatoes, lentils and stock. Season with ground black pepper. Bring to the boil and simmer for about 40 minutes. The lentils should be tender and the liquid reduced to just coat the lentils. Season with salt before serving.

VARIATIONS
- Add 1 fresh chilli, deseeded and finely chopped (see page 15), when the garlic is added.
- Stir in 1 tablespoon chopped, fresh coriander at the end.

GRILLED RADICCHIO

1 head radicchio
1 tablespoon olive oil
freshly ground black pepper
3 or 4 anchovy fillets
chopped parsley
1 tablespoon grated Parmesan cheese

1. Heat the grill to its highest temperature. Cut the radicchio into wedges. Place on the grill rack and brush with half the oil. Season with black pepper and grill for a few minutes until tender and charred at the edges.
2. Meanwhile, chop the anchovy fillets and mix with the parsley and remaining oil.
3. Put the radicchio on a plate. Pour the anchovy dressing on top and sprinkle with Parmesan cheese. Serve immediately.

BAKED BLUE CHEESE MUSHROOMS

This dish can be used as a first course, a quick snack served with crusty bread to mop up the savoury juices, or as an accompaniment to a main course.

2 large flat mushrooms, wiped clean
15g/½oz butter, melted
salt and freshly ground black pepper
lemon juice
55g/2oz blue Brie or Cambozola, diced
extra butter for greasing

1. Set the oven to 190°C/375°F/gas mark 5. Brush the mushrooms with melted butter. Season with a little salt, plenty of ground black pepper and lemon juice. Bake for 10 minutes.
2. Put the diced cheese inside the mushrooms. Return to the oven for 5–10 minutes, until the cheese has melted and the mushrooms are tender.

VARIATION
Baked Garlic Mushrooms: Instead of using blue cheese, simply add a crushed garlic clove to the melted butter.

GRATED COURGETTE AND CARROT

1 small carrot
½ courgette
15g/½oz butter
salt and freshly ground black pepper
squeeze of lime juice

1. Peel and coarsely grate the carrot. Wash and grate the courgette
2. Melt the butter in a heavy-based frying pan. When foaming, add the vegetables. Season with salt and pepper and sauté for a few minutes until softened. Add a squeeze of lime juice and mix well before serving.

VARIATION
Stir in 1 teaspoon sultanas and 2 teaspoons crème fraîche just before serving.

PIZZA

This recipe uses a home-made base but ready-made bases will do nearly as well. The quantities given make a 12-inch pizza.

SERVES 1–2
For the base:
170g/6oz strong or plain white flour
1 level teaspoon easy-blend dried yeast
110ml/4 fl oz warm water
2 teaspoons sunflower or olive oil

For the topping:
225g/8oz tin chopped tomatoes
pinch dried basil or oregano
2 tablespoons olive oil
1 garlic clove, crushed
salt and freshly ground black pepper

1. Put the flour into a mixing bowl and make a well in the centre. Place the yeast, water and oil in the well. Mix together to a soft dough and knead for 5 minutes. Place in a clean bowl, cover and leave in a warm place until doubled in size.

2. Make the topping: put the tomatoes into a small pan with the herbs, 1 tablespoon of oil and the garlic. Season and simmer for 10 minutes until slightly reduced and thickened.

3. Set the oven to 230°C/450°F/gas mark 8. Knead the dough on a floured surface and roll out to a 30cm/12 inch circle. Spread the topping over the dough, adding any extras you like (see below). Drizzle with the remaining olive

oil. Bake in the preheated oven for 15–20 minutes, or until the crust is brown and the top melted.

EXTRA TOPPINGS

Mushroom and Mozzarella: Scatter 55g/2oz sliced mushrooms over the tomato sauce. Top with 140g/5oz sliced mozzarella, and 1 teaspoon grated Parmesan cheese. Season with salt and ground black pepper and a pinch of dried oregano.

Grilled Vegetables: Deseed and quarter 1 red pepper, and slice 1 small courgette. Brush with 1 tablespoon olive oil and grill until dark brown. Remove the skin from the pepper and slice thickly. Arrange the vegetable slices on the pizza. Dot with black olives, 55g/2oz goats' cheese and sprinkle with 55g/2oz grated mozzarella. Season with salt and ground black pepper.

Spinach, Pinenuts and Raisins: Make 1 quantity spinach, pinenut and raisin accompaniment for pasta (see page 63). Spoon on top of the pizza. Sprinkle with 85g/3oz grated mozzarella and 1 teaspoon grated Parmesan cheese.

Avocado and Salami: Arrange 85g/3oz sliced German or Italian salami on the pizza base. Stone, peel and slice 1 small, ripe avocado pear. Arrange on top of the salami. Season with salt and ground black pepper. Cover with 85g/3oz grated mozzarella.

SAUCES &
ACCOMPANIMENTS

SAUCES AND ACCOMPANIMENTS

Good sauces, stocks and dressings enhance almost any dish, and they are not difficult to make. Equally useful and easy to prepare are flavoured butters and spice mixtures. All are described in this section. If you've never baked your own bread, try the quick recipe on page 167 – it really couldn't be easier and will give you immense satisfaction, as well as a delicious accompaniment to your meals.
All recipes serve 1 unless stated otherwise.

MAYONNAISE

2 egg yolks
salt and pepper
1 teaspoon pale mustard
290ml/½ pint olive oil, or 150ml/¼ pint
each olive and salad oil
squeeze of lemon juice
1 tablespoon wine vinegar

1. Put the yolks into a bowl with a pinch of salt and the mustard and beat well with a wooden spoon.
2. Add the oil, literally drop by drop, beating all the time. The mixture should be very thick by the time half the oil is added.
3. Beat in the lemon juice.
4. Resume pouring in the oil, going rather more confidently now, but alternating the dribbles of oil with small quantities of vinegar.

5. Add salt and pepper to taste. Store in an airtight jar and refrigerate.

NOTE: If the mixture curdles, another egg yolk should be beaten in a separate bowl, and the curdled mixture beaten drop by drop into it.

TARTARE SAUCE

1 tablespoon mayonnaise
1 teaspoon chopped parsley
1 spring onion, chopped
squeeze of lemon juice
salt and freshly ground black pepper

Mix all the ingredients together and
season to taste.

VARIATION

Add 1 teaspoon chopped, rinsed
gherkins or rinsed capers to the
mixture.

WHITE SAUCE

This is a quick and easy basic sauce
15g/½oz butter
1 rounded teaspoon flour
pinch dry mustard
150ml/¼ pint creamy milk
salt and white pepper

1. Melt the butter in a heavy-based
saucepan.
2. Add the flour and the mustard and
stir over the heat for 1 minute. Draw the
pan off the heat, pour in the milk and
mix well.
3. Return the sauce to the heat and stir
continually until boiling.
4. Simmer for 2–3 minutes and season
with salt and pepper.

CHEESE SAUCE

15g/½oz butter
1 rounded teaspoon flour
pinch dry English mustard
pinch cayenne pepper
150ml/¼ pint milk
55g/2oz Gruyère or strong Cheddar
cheese, grated
30g/1oz Parmesan cheese, grated
salt and pepper

1. Melt the butter and stir in the flour, mustard and cayenne pepper. Cook, stirring, for 1 minute. Draw the pan off the heat. Pour in the milk and mix well.
2. Return the pan to the heat and stir until boiling. Simmer, stirring well, for 2 minutes.
3. Add all the cheese and mix well, but do not re-boil.
4. Season with salt and pepper as necessary.

QUICK HOLLANDAISE SAUCE

SERVES 1–2
1 tablespoon wine vinegar
2 peppercorns
1 bayleaf
2 teaspoons water
1 egg yolk
45g/1½oz unsalted, softened butter
lemon juice
salt

1. Put the vinegar, peppercorns, bayleaf and water into a small pan and boil until reduced by half (it will take only seconds). Remove the peppercorns and bayleaf.
2. Remove from the heat and whisk in the egg yolk until thick and fluffy.
3. Return to a gentle heat and gradually whisk in the softened butter a little at a time. Remove from the heat if the sauce gets more than warm. Add the lemon juice and salt to taste.

VARIATION
Add 1 tablespoon chopped fresh herbs such as chives, chervil or tarragon.

TOMATO SAUCE

SERVES 2
1 tablespoon olive oil
½ small onion, finely chopped
1 garlic clove, crushed
225g/8oz tin chopped tomatoes
salt and freshly ground black pepper
½ tablespoon dried basil
pinch sugar
lemon juice

1. Heat the oil and sweat the onion gently until soft. Add the garlic and cook for 1 further minute. Stir in the tomatoes and season with salt, pepper and basil. Simmer for 20 minutes.
2. Check for seasoning, then add the sugar and lemon juice. The sauce can be served as it is or liquidized and reheated.

TOMATO AND DILL SAUCE

This is a cold sauce which can be served with grilled fish or poultry.

SERVES 1–2
2 tablespoons fromage frais
1 tablespoon finely chopped dill
1 tomato, peeled, deseeded and chopped
salt and freshly ground black pepper
lemon juice

1. Mix all the ingredients together and season with salt, pepper and lemon juice. Allow to stand for 10 minutes before serving.

SALSAS

These recipes are for fresh Latin American sauces, and their tantalizing flavours are quite addictive. They can be the lone cook's best friend, transforming a humble grilled chicken breast into a gourmet feast, or making a quick hors d'oeuvres when served with tortilla chips. The combinations of ingredients in salsas are infinite, but all should be based on fresh chilli, chopped onion, lime juice and fresh coriander. After that, anything goes. The recipes below are quite mild, but add as many chillies as you like.

TOMATO SALSA

1 ripe beefsteak tomato
1 fresh green chilli (see page 15)
1 teaspoon finely chopped onion
juice of ½ lime
salt and freshly ground black pepper
pinch ground cumin
1 tablespoon chopped fresh coriander

1. Chop the tomato. Carefully deseed and finely chop the chilli. Mix together with the onion and lime juice.
2. Season with plenty of salt, a little black pepper and the cumin. Stir in the coriander. Leave to stand for 10 minutes before serving.

VARIATIONS
- Substitute the coriander with chopped fresh mint.
- Add ½ or whole small, ripe avocado, stoned, peeled and chopped.

ORANGE SALSA

1 orange
1 fresh red chilli (see page 15)
¼ red onion, finely chopped
squeeze of lime juice
1 tablespoon chopped fresh coriander
salt and freshly ground black pepper

1. Peel the orange as you would an apple. Cut into segments, removing all the pith and seeds. Squeeze the pithy remains over a mixing bowl to extract the juice. Chop the segments and add to the juice.
2. Carefully deseed and chop the chilli. Mix with the orange and stir in the onion, lime juice and coriander. Season with plenty of salt and a little pepper. Allow to stand for 10 minutes before serving.

VARIATIONS
- Substitute the orange with 1 tablespoon lime juice and ½ mango, stoned, peeled and finely chopped.
- Substitute the orange with 1 tablespoon orange juice and 1 small banana, peeled and finely chopped.

CHICKEN STOCK

onion, *sliced*
celery, *sliced*
carrot, *sliced*
chicken bones
parsley
thyme
bay leaf
peppercorns

1. Put all the ingredients into a saucepan. Cover generously with water and bring to the boil slowly. Skim off any fat and/or scum.
2. Simmer for 3–4 hours, skimming frequently and topping up the water level if necessary. The liquid should reduce to half the original quantity.
3. Strain, cool and lift off all the fat.

FISH STOCK

onion, *sliced*
carrot, *sliced*
celery, *sliced*
fish bones, skins, fins, heads or tails,
crustacean shells (e.g. prawn shells,
mussel shells, etc.)
parsley stalks
bay leaf
pinch fresh thyme
pepper

1. Put all the ingredients together in a pan, with water to cover, and bring to the boil. Turn down to simmer and skim off any scum.
2. Simmer for 20 minutes if the fish bones are small, 30 minutes if large. Strain.

NOTE: The flavour of fish stock is impaired if the bones are cooked for too long. Once strained however, it may be strengthened by further boiling and reducing.

VEGETABLE STOCK

This recipe makes 290–425ml/½–¾ pint of stock.

2 tablespoons sunflower oil
1 onion, roughly chopped
1 leek, roughly chopped
1 large carrot, roughly chopped
2 celery sticks, roughly chopped
few cabbage leaves, shredded
few mushroom stalks
2 garlic cloves, crushed
few parsley stalks
6 black peppercorns
sea salt
1 large bay leaf
6 tablespoons white wine
570ml/1 pint water

1. Heat the oil in a large pan. Add the vegetables, garlic and parsley, then cover and cook gently for 5 minutes until softened.
2. Add the peppercorns, salt, bay leaf, wine and water and bring to the boil. Reduce the heat and simmer for 30 minutes, or until the liquid has reduced by half.
3. Strain the stock through a sieve and discard the vegetable pulp. Allow to cool. Skim off any fat. Use as required.

NOTE: The stock can be kept, covered, in the refrigerator for one week. It can also be frozen.

FRENCH DRESSING (VINAIGRETTE)

3 tablespoons salad oil
1 tablespoon wine vinegar
salt and pepper

1. Put all the ingredients into a screw-top jar. Before using, shake until well emulsified.

VARIATION
This dressing can be flavoured with crushed garlic, mustard, a pinch of sugar, chopped fresh herbs, etc., as desired.

NOTE: If kept refrigerated, the dressing will more easily form an emulsion when whisked or shaken, and has a slightly thicker consistency.

TOMATO AND PEPPER DRESSING

½ red pepper
2 tomatoes, peeled and deseeded
1 teaspoon finely chopped red onion
1 tablespoon olive oil
juice of ½ lemon
salt and freshly ground black pepper
pinch cayenne pepper

1. Heat the grill to its highest temperature. Remove the membrane and seeds from the pepper. Grill, skin side up, until black and blistered. Cool, then remove the skin with a sharp knife. Finely chop the flesh.
2. Chop the tomato finely and mix with the onion and red pepper. Whisk together the oil and lemon juice. Pour over the tomato mixture and season with salt, pepper and cayenne. Leave to stand for 1 hour before serving.

FLAVOURED BUTTERS

Flavoured butters are very useful for livening up plain grilled meat or fish, or for adding interest to rice, couscous or baked potatoes. The butter may be served in soft spoonfuls, or rolled into a cylinder and wrapped with foil or damp greaseproof paper, then chilled and sliced as required. If it is to be kept for more than two days, it should be frozen. For a special occasion, pipe the butter in whirls on to greaseproof paper and freeze. Remove from the freezer 5 minutes before serving. Place a whirl of butter on top of hot food and it will melt prettily at the edges when the dish is served.

Lime butter: Mix zest and juice of ½ lime, 1 teaspoon chopped chives, salt and freshly ground black pepper into 30g/1oz softened butter.

Cumin butter: Mix 1 teaspoon ground cumin, squeeze of lemon, salt and freshly ground black pepper into 30g/1oz softened butter.

Stilton butter: Mix 15g/½oz grated Stilton and freshly ground black pepper into 30g/1oz softened butter.

Mustard and Mint butter: Mix 2 teaspoons wholegrain mustard, squeeze of lemon juice and 1 heaped teaspoon chopped, fresh mint into 30g/1oz softened butter.

Chilli and Coriander butter: Mix teaspoon finely chopped onion, 1 green chilli, deseeded and finely chopped (see page 15), squeeze of lime juice and 1 tablespoon chopped fresh coriander into 30g/1oz softened butter.

Sun-dried Tomato butter: Mix 2 teaspoons red pesto or sun-dried tomato paste into 30g/1oz softened butter.

Avocado butter: This should be made in a food processor. Whizz together 30g/1oz soft butter, ½ ripe avocado pear, peeled and stoned, juice of ½ lemon, salt, pepper and a dash of Tabasco sauce.

CURRY POWDER

There is no beating freshly made curry powder. The art of making a good one is in toasting all the spices; when the seeds are split by the heat, their full flavour comes through. Take care not to burn the seeds or the powder will taste bitter. This mixture, which is quite hot, can be used for all the recipes in this book specifying curry powder. To increase or lessen the heat, adjust the quantity of chillies accordingly.

To keep the curry powder fresh it is best stored in the freezer or a cool, dark place. Use within 3 months; any longer and the spices lose their flavour.

This quantity makes enough powder for several curries; halve the amount of spices to make a smaller quantity. The spices can be bought from specialist grocers and some supermarkets.

6 tablespoons coriander seeds.
4 tablespoons cumin seeds
6 dried red chillies
1 tablespoon black peppercorns
1 tablespoon mustard seeds, preferably black
3 tablespoons ground turmeric
3 teaspoons ground fenugreek

1. Heat a large frying pan. Add the coriander seeds and toss and toast over a medium heat until they begin to pop and colour. Transfer to a plate to cool.
2. Add the cumin seeds and chillies and toast in the same way until the cumin pops and the chillies turn dark reddish-brown in colour. Add them to the coriander and allow to cool.
3. Toast the peppercorns and mustard seeds individually in the same way and allow to cool.
4. When all the seeds are cold, put into a spice/coffee grinder or mortar. Pound together until a fine powder is formed. Stir the turmeric and fenugreek into the powder. Transfer to an airtight container and store until required.

GARAM MASALA

Garam masala (literally 'mixed spice') does not store well, so it is best made fresh. This recipe makes about 3 tablespoons. Keep any excess in an airtight container in a cool, dark place, or freeze it.

20 cardamom pods
5cm/2 inch piece cinnamon stick
1 teaspoon cumin seeds
1 teaspoon whole cloves
1 teaspoon whole black peppercorns
1 teaspoon fenugreek seeds
½ teaspoon freshly grated nutmeg
½ teaspoon chilli powder

1. Break open the cardamom pods and remove the seeds.
2. Put all the spices in a spice/coffee grinder and whizz to a fine powder. Store in an airtight container until required.

QUICK BREAD

340g/12oz strong white flour or granary wholemeal flour
large pinch salt
3g/½ sachet easy-blend dried yeast
2 teaspoons sunflower oil
225ml/8 fl oz warm water
milk for glazing
sesame or poppy seeds

1. Preheat the oven to 220°C/425°F/gas mark 7.
2. Put the flour and salt into a mixing bowl and make a well in the centre. Place the yeast, oil and water in the well.
3. Mix to a soft dough. If the dough is too sticky, add a little more flour; if it is too dry, add extra warm water. Knead for about 5 minutes or until smooth and elastic.
4. Roll the dough into a long loaf shape and place on an oiled baking sheet. Cover and leave in a warm place to rise until doubled in size. Brush the top with milk and scatter with sesame or poppy seeds. Bake for about 30 minutes. The loaf is ready when it sounds hollow if tapped on the underside.

VARIATION
Shape the dough into about six rolls and bake for 20 minutes.

TOMATO AND BASIL BRUSCHETTA

1 mini French stick or 15cm/6 inch piece
of French bread
1 garlic clove, peeled
1 ripe tomato, peeled, deseeded and
chopped
6 basil leaves, torn
salt and freshly ground black pepper
1 tablespoon olive oil

1. Heat the grill to high. Cut the bread in half lengthways and toast on the cut side only. With a wide-bladed knife, crush the garlic and rub it over the toasted side of the bread.
2. Mix together the tomato and basil and season with salt and pepper. Spread the mixture over the bread, dribble with olive oil and grill for a few minutes until the tomato is hot and the bread crisp.

VARIATION
Spread the bread with red pesto, top with mild goat's cheese and grill.

OLIVE OIL BREAD

1 mini French stick or 15cm/6 inch piece
of French bread
1 garlic clove, peeled (optional)
2 teaspoons olive oil

1. Cut the bread in half lengthways. Crush the garlic with a wide-bladed knife and rub over the bread.
2. Heat a heavy frying pan or cast-iron skillet. Brush the olive oil over the cut side of the bread. Toast cut-side down on the skillet until crisp in the middle and charred at the edges.

DUMPLINGS

30g/1oz self-raising flour
15g/½oz shredded suet
salt and freshly ground black pepper
1–2 tablespoons water

1. Mix all the ingredients together and bind to a stiffish dough with the water. It should be of a consistency that will fall reluctantly from a spoon. Season with salt and pepper.
2. Form the dough into one or two dumplings and add to a simmering soup or casserole. Cook for 10 minutes covered and 10 minutes uncovered.

VARIATIONS
Add any of the following ingredients to the flour.
- 1 teaspoon chopped fresh parsley
- 1 level tablespoon grated Parmesan cheese
- good pinch caraway seeds
- 1 teaspoon horseradish relish

DESSERTS

DESSERTS

Fresh fruit, flavoured yoghurts, Greek yoghurt and honey, ice-cream or a ripe cheese are perfectly satisfying desserts for everyday eating. But there are occasions when something more indulgent is desired, and this is the time to use this section of the book. Even if you are a solitary pudding lover, the recipes that make more than one serving keep well if covered and refrigerated.

Coffee is always a good finale to a meal. For maximum freshness buy ground coffee from specialist shops rather than supermarkets because they sell it in smaller quantities. Store it in an airtight container. Alternatively, buy coffee beans and grind them freshly as required.

Cafetières are available in one-person sizes, as are Moka Express coffee-makers. The latter make a really good attempt at espresso-style coffee.

All recipes serve 1 unless stated otherwise.

SIMPLE STRAWBERRY ICE-CREAM

This wonderfully simple ice-cream freezes beautifully with no regular beatings. It works equally well using a large, ripe mango.

SERVES 4
340g/12oz strawberries
290ml/½ pint double cream
110g/4oz caster sugar
4 tablespoons advocaat
squeeze of lemon juice

1. Hull and wash the strawberries. Purée in a liquidizer or food processor.
2. Whip the double cream lightly. Fold in the caster sugar, advocaat and lastly the strawberry purée. Check for sweetness and add more sugar if necessary. (Remember that the ice-cream will taste less sweet when frozen, so err on the generous side.) Add a squeeze of lemon juice.
3. Put the ice-cream into a shallow, covered container and freeze overnight. Remove from the freezer 30 minutes before using.

TOFFEE PECAN BANANAS

1 banana
15g/½oz butter
15g/½oz pecan nuts, roughly chopped
15g/½oz soft, light brown sugar
2 tablespoons water
pinch grated lime zest

To serve:
vanilla ice-cream

1. Peel the banana and cut in half lengthways.
2. Melt the butter in a frying pan. Add the banana and nuts and turn in the butter. Add the sugar and water, then heat slowly until dissolved and the mixture is bubbling.
3. Add the lime zest. Turn the banana in the toffee sauce and serve with ice-cream.

CHOCOLATE TRUFFLE POT

2 ratafia biscuits or 1 sponge finger broken into four
1 teaspoon brandy
30g/1oz dark chocolate, broken up
60ml/2 fl oz double cream

1. Put the ratafia biscuits in the bottom of a ramekin dish. Sprinkle the brandy over them.
2. Melt the chocolate in a basin positioned over, not in, a pan of simmering water. Allow to cool but not set.
3. Whip the cream lightly and reserve 1 teaspoonful. Fold the remaining cream into the cooled chocolate. Spoon this mixture on top of the ratafia biscuits. Chill until set. Serve with the reserved whipped cream on top.

NOTE: Rum, Grand Marnier, Cointreau or sherry can be substituted for the brandy.

PEARS SAVOYARD

1 large, firm pear
15g/½oz butter
1 teaspoon caster sugar
2 tablespoons double cream
squeeze of lemon juice

1. Remove the skin from the pear using a potato peeler. Cut the flesh into eighths and slice away the core.
2. Melt the butter in a heavy-based frying pan. Add the pear pieces and fry gently for a few minutes until tender.
3. Add the sugar and allow to dissolve. Stir in the double cream, bring to the boil and add a squeeze of lemon juice.

MARMALADE PUDDING

SERVES 2
butter for greasing
1 orange
1 tablespoon orange marmalade
knob of butter
55g/2oz soft butter
55g/2oz caster sugar
55g/2oz self-raising flour
1 egg

To serve:
English egg custard (see page 178) or vanilla ice-cream

1. Grease a 570ml/1 pint ovenproof dish. Using a sharp knife, peel the orange as you would an apple, removing all the pith and peel and saving any juice. Cut the orange into slices, discarding any pips. Arrange the slices in an overlapping layer in the prepared dish.
2. Put the marmalade into a small saucepan with the knob of butter. Place over the heat and stir until boiling. Pour over the orange slices.
3. Set the oven to 190°C/375°F/gas mark 5. Put the butter, sugar, flour and egg into a mixing bowl with the reserved orange juice. Beat until light and fluffy. Spread on top of the marmalade base.
4. Bake for about 30 minutes until golden brown and firm when pressed with the fingertips. Loosen round the edges with a knife and turn on to a serving dish. Serve with custard or ice-cream.

BAKED STUFFED APPLE

1 large cooking apple
1 tablespoon dried fruit, such as
sultanas, currants, figs or apricots
1 teaspoon honey
2 tablespoons orange juice

To serve:
English egg custard (see page 178)

1. Wash the apple and remove the core with an apple corer. With a sharp knife, score the skin round the middle of the apple. Set the oven to 180°C/350°F/gas mark 4.
2. If using dried figs or apricots, cut to about the same size as sultanas. Mix the dried fruit with the honey and spoon firmly into the centre of the apple.
3. Spoon over the orange juice. Bake for about 40 minutes, basting occasionally. The apples should be soft right the way through when tested with a skewer. Serve with English egg custard.

DIPPING CREAM FOR FRESH FRUIT

2 tablespoons Greek yoghurt or sieved
cottage cheese
2 tablespoons double cream, lightly
whipped
2 teaspoons muscovado sugar

To serve:
wedges of fresh fruit

1. Fold the yoghurt or cottage cheese into the whipped cream. Sprinkle with the muscovado sugar.
2. Leave the cream to stand for 3–4 hours to allow the sugar to dissolve. Serve with wedges of fresh fruit or whole berries.

VARIATION
Instead of muscovado sugar, use the zest and juice of ½ lime and icing sugar to taste. Mix together and leave to stand for 30 minutes before serving.

GRILLED NECTARINES

This dish works well, even if the nectarines are not quite ripe.

1 nectarine
30g/1oz fresh cherries, redcurrants or
black berries
1 tablespoon white wine or orange juice
15g/½oz caster sugar

To serve:
strawberry or mango ice-cream (see
page 173)

1. Heat the grill to high. Cut the nectarine in half and remove the stone. Place cut side up in an ovenproof dish.
2. Halve and stone the cherries. Destalk the redcurrants or black berries. Wash the fruit and scatter over the nectarine halves.
3. Spoon over the wine, then sprinkle evenly with the sugar. Grill for 5–10 minutes. Serve hot, warm or chilled with a helping of ice-cream.

GRILLED BERRY MERINGUE

SERVES 2
85g/3oz frozen summer fruit
2 tablespoons apple juice
1 teaspoon sherry
2 trifle sponges
150ml/¼ pint double cream
1 egg white
55g/2oz caster sugar

1. Place the frozen fruit in a bowl, spoon the apple juice and sherry over it and leave to defrost. Arrange the trifle sponges in the base of a 570ml/1 pint soufflé dish and add the defrosted fruit and all the juice.
2. Whip the cream lightly and spread over the fruit.
3. Heat the grill to high. Whisk the egg white until stiff. Add half the sugar and continue to whisk until very stiff and shiny. Fold in the remaining sugar.
4. Spread the meringue over the whipped cream, leaving a rough surface. Grill for a few minutes until browned on top. (This happens quickly, so keep watching.) Allow to cool before serving.

ENGLISH EGG CUSTARD

1 egg yolk
2 teaspoons caster sugar
½ teaspoon cornflour
150ml/¼ pint creamy milk
2 drops vanilla essence

1. Beat together the egg yolk, sugar and cornflour.
2. Bring the milk slowly to the boil. Pour on to the egg yolk mixture, stirring steadily. Mix well.
3. Pour the custard back into the pan and stir over a gentle heat until the mixture thickens so that it will coat the back of a spoon. Add the vanilla essence.

NOTE: For an extra rich custard, stir in 2 tablespoons double cream with the vanilla.

SULTANA LOAF

This is a simple cake recipe that can easily be consumed by one or two people in a matter of a few days. However, if need be, it does keep well in an airtight container for up to two weeks, or can be frozen. Serve plain or spread with butter.

butter for greasing
170g/6oz self-raising flour (½ wholemeal, ½ white flour if you like)
85g/3oz butter
55g/2oz sultanas
85g/3oz brown sugar
1 teaspoon mixed spice
1 tablespoon marmalade
1 egg
2 tablespoons orange juice
12 whole pecan nuts or unblanched almonds

1. Cut a piece of greaseproof paper to fit the base of a 450g/1lb loaf tin. Grease the tin with butter or oil, fit the greaseproof paper in the bottom and grease the paper too. Set the oven to 190°C/375°F/gas mark 5.
2. Put the flour in a bowl and rub in the butter until the mixture resembles fine breadcrumbs. Stir in the sultanas, sugar and spice.
3. Bind the mixture with the marmalade, egg and orange juice to a reluctant dropping consistency.
4. Spoon into the loaf tin, spreading the top evenly. Arrange the nuts on top and bake for about 40 minutes, until well risen, golden brown and firm to touch.

CHOCOLATE CHIP OAT COOKIES

55g/2oz lard or solid vegetable oil
55g/2oz butter or margarine
85g/3oz caster sugar
1 teaspoon golden syrup
110g/4oz self-raising flour
1 teaspoon bicarbonate of soda
55g/2oz rolled oats
1 teaspoon vanilla essence
1 tablespoon boiling water
55g/2oz chocolate chips

1. Grease a baking sheet. Set the oven to 180°C/350°F/gas mark 4.
2. Beat together the lard, butter, sugar and syrup until light and creamy.
3. Add the flour, bicarbonate of soda and oats and mix well. Add the vanilla essence, water and chocolate chips. Carefully mix to a firm paste.
4. Roll the paste into balls about the size of a walnut, and place on the baking sheet. Leave plenty of space between the balls as they will spread out during cooking.
5. Bake for 15 minutes until golden brown. They will still be soft. Leave to cool for a little while before lifting on to a wire rack to cool.

INDEX